The
PONDERING
POLE

Ed Poniewaz

2016-2019

0|6|2021

To Keith,

now thyself through thy ancestry!

[signature]

The Pondering Pole
2016—2019

© 2021 by Ed Poniewaz

ISBN: 978-1-63110-484-8

Cover Photos by Linsey Shekas

Printed in the United States of America by
Graphic Connections Group Publishing
Chesterfield, Missouri 63005

Contents

Section I. Introduction 1

Section II. 2016 5

February 2016 **All You Need is Love** 7

March 2016 **A Polish Pro-lifer** 11

April 2016 **Poland Charting** 14

June 2016 **The Chico Marx Effect** 18

July 2016 **"Let democracy work in Poland."** 22

August 2016 **When Traveling Through St. Louis This Summer** . . . 25

September 2016 **California (and Polish) Dream'n** 28

October 2016 **Something There is That Doesn't Love a Wall** 30

November 2016 **Count The Fingers and Toes** 33

December 2016 **Cultivating a "Cultural" Inheritance** 36

Section III. 2017 39

January 2017 **Web Enabled** 41

February 2017 **Good vs. Evil** 44

March 2017 **Come Home** 47

April 2017 **Make it Better** 50

May 2017 **A Classless America? A Classless Polonia?** 53

June 2017 **"Our meeting place... "** 56

July 2017 **Gamers w Polsce (in Polish)** 59

August 2017 **All About the Cause!** 62

September 2017 **Why Polish?** 65

October 2017 **Heritage for a Day, Month, or Lifetime** 70

November 2017 **Poloni... What?** 72

December 2017 **Christmas Musing and Giving, Giving and Musing** . 75

Section IV. 2018 77

January 2018 **On the Greatest List.** 79

February 2018 **Which leads to...** 82

March 2018 **So Good, So Good, So Good!!!** 85

April 2018 **... but words will never hurt me.** 90

May 2018 **Boys will be boys?** 94

June 2018 **The story behind the story.** 98

July 2018 **"Strictly Polish – polkas, obereks, and waltzes."** 101

August 2018 **"... This is the real thing."** 104

September 2018 **On the list.** 107

October 2018 **A need for culture?** 110

November 2018 **The other guy.** 114

December 2018 **Sometimes dreams do come true.** 117

Section V. 2019 121

January 2019 **That's What I'm Talking About!** 123

February 2019 **A Medley of Inspiration** 126

March 2019 **Where is the Polish Architectural Capital?** 129

April 2019 **Go West, Young Pan!.** 132

May 2019 **Born in Poland** 137

June 2019 **"Start with the Positive Things."** 141

July 2019 **The Study of "Us."** 144

August 2019 **Reparations or Restorations?** 148

September 2019 **In Heaven, There Must Be Chupaj Siupaj** 151

October 2019 **Bitter or Better?** .154

November 2019 **Definitely Not Commando** 157

Section VI. Dziekuje Bardzo! 161

I

Introduction

Introduction

*O*ver fifteen years ago, I discovered the *Polish American Journal* published out of Buffalo, New York. I was very impressed with this monthly newspaper for Polish Americans and approached the editor with an idea for a column that would be about famous, successful, or important Americans or others that have a Polish background or connection but were not familiar or even known to Poles or non-Poles either because they lived under a changed name or their importance was not apparent or even recognized. He thought the idea was a good one and gave me the name for the column: *The Pondering Pole.*

My goal with every *Pondering Pole* was to educate the reader and give them something uplifting and positive about being Polish. I believe that American Polonia has lost two to three generations to shame, despair, or ignorance related to their ethnic ancestry or how this or that culture was more preferred or "better" than Polish. Identifying important or successful persons, places, or events that have a Polish connection was a way to give those in the Polish community information that would renew their faith in their Polish background and allow them to feel comfortable in their own skin and understand what it means to be Polish.

The format of the column was first to highlight and present the famous, successful, or important person in the body of the column, and then mention or ask in the following section whether another person or persons had a Polish background or connection called, "Polish or Not?" This is where I summoned (and hoped for) the research and knowledge of the readers to help me reveal someone's Polishness. The final paragraph usually closed with a mention of the monthly Polish holiday or current event and sometimes a one or two sentence recap of the main topic and then a thank you to any readers or others that contributed to the column. Lastly, always I asked, if "you have a thought about this month's topic, have a question, or have interesting facts to share" to write or eMail me. I did not get a lot of feedback but when I did hear from someone it was encouraging, made me think I was accomplishing something, and just made me feel good. It is fun to hear from the audience, good or bad.

As time went on the focus of the first and primary part changed from a life story of so-and-so to instead a general idea or a topic of a Polish nature. Sometimes the idea or topic could stand on its own or frequently I would use this as a way to weave a person, place, or event with a Polish connection into the piece as an example in support of or to accompany the message.

I began writing the *Pondering Pole* in 2005 but this book is a compilation of articles from the years 2016 through 2019. Perhaps I can do other editions to include other years or maybe a "best of" version in the future. We shall see.

My hope is that the purpose of the *Pondering Pole* is realized for some and if that was not accomplished, this project (or experiment) was a selfish way for me to understand how my ethnicity shaped me and to understand other cultures. Culture comparison is a good thing and rather than grade one against the other, it makes for a more healthy and grounded perspective of other people, their history, and their culture. It has been a wonderful experience and adventure. I recommend you do the same.

Please note that some of the references to people, places, and events have changed since the creation of this book. Some of the places no longer exist and some of the events are no longer scheduled. That is life in an ethnic community as places, traditions, rituals, and gatherings change. Life changes. Some of the articles that originally appeared in the *Polish American Journal* have been updated as well. Some did not appear in the *Journal*, but are included in this book.

I hope you enjoy *The Pondering Pole, 2016-2019.*

II

2016

February 2016

All You Need is Love

As John Lennon and John Paul II would tell us…

The panelist Pat Buchanan of *The McLaughlin Group* (a weekly public affairs program) made the prediction for 2016 that the flow of refugees into Europe will not subside. Even as an American an ocean away, the thought of that makes me apprehensive.

There is love and then there is tough love. What does Poland do with the refugees streaming in from the turmoil in the Middle East and is this situation different from others? Living amongst other cultures is nothing new for the Poles. The decades before World War II the ethnic makeup of Poland included large numbers of Germans, Lithuanians, Jews, Gypsies, Tartars, Ukrainians, and others.

The rearranged border and transfer of people after the war made the country more homogeneous than it had ever been. Each world crisis has its own characteristics and circumstances and the Poles need to evaluate what is in their best interest while maintaining proportional moral sympathy and support. Security, resources, and accommodation are important considerations. I am confident the Poles will work it out for all concerned but let's see what happens.

Talking about refugees and the kindness of Poles to strangers brings me to the next topic. Got an eMail from Frank J. Nice (yes, that is his name folks; the original Polish name was Nye) responding to my call for examples of Polish names for kids and grandkids. Frank's daughter is Melania and the etymological description of the name shows the Polish pronunciation first (before the other primary links to the word - Italian, Spanish, and Late Roman) so we can conclude that Polish is the root or near root for this name. Americans are familiar with "Melanie" that most likely comes from the Polish Melania rather than the reverse. As Frank also told me, he saw it on a stained glass window in a Polish church in Maine. His other kids have Polish variants Eryk (for Eric) and Liana (pronounced the Polish way lee-ah-na).

You can argue that excellent naming is Frank's main claim to fame but like Seinfeld's pocket calculator "it does other things!!" Frank is a pharmacist (with degrees all the way up to doctor), author, and a humanitarian. Let me tell you about what he has done in his life, for Polonia, and for all of us.

Frank along with his wife Myung Hee have written a book *The Galactagogue Recipe Book*, (Hale Publishing, 2014) geared "For nursing mothers leading modern stress-filled lives," it is a collection of recipes that offer real nutritional support, are comprised mostly of inexpensive food easily found in most grocery stores, and are simple to prepare. Unique characteristics of this book are the catering to breastfeeding women, the use of herbs, spices, and foods traditionally used to support milk supply, and a number of the dishes are family or Polish or Korean "ancestors' recipes." This is the perfect shower or pregnant mother gift and for more information visit www.nicebreastfeeding.com.

Writing a recipe book is a great way to "serve" humanity but in a continuing eMail conversation he shared with me his involvement with the ongoing reconstruction in Haiti called "Health and Education for Haiti" that has lasted for 20 years:

As a pharmacist, I started a medical mission to Haiti 20 years ago. We continue to go, now three times a year several weeks each time. When we are there, we see 1,000 or more patients per week. We have established several clinics in Haiti with ongoing care when even we are not in Haiti. I have been to Haiti 20 times so far and will be going next in January 2016. I also started a school in Haiti for poor and orphan children.

Frank is on the board of directors for the charity and you can learn more about it at www.hehonline.org. Service to others is such a noble and worthy vocation and we admire Frank and his family for all that they do for people in whatever form that takes.

A Polish Blessing

I am the father of two beautiful daughters and the youngest one was married November 14, 2015. Brigette Aniela Poniewaz and Alexander Richter Schubert made a life commitment to each other and I am so happy for these two kind, intelligent, and gentle souls. May God bless them and keep them safe (or in Polish - Moze Bog im blogoslawil I zapewnic im bezpiedzenstwo.)

Polish or Not?

The show *Strange Inheritance* featured a taxidermy business in transition begun by a man named Steve Kulash. Now deceased, Steve Kulash was well known in Hollywood and elsewhere for the beautiful and realistic work he and his sons produced. Check out episode 25 "Masters of Taxidermy" and the "legendary Vancover taxidermy shop" (http://www.strangeinheritance.com/episodeguide). Steve Kulash, Polish or not?

In the April 2013 issue of the Polish American Journal, the Pondering Pole asked if Chris Botti, the super smooth jazz trumpet player and friend of Poland was Polish because of his classical piano playing mother. In a recent EthniCelebs post, Chris is Italian on his father's side and mom comes in as English, Scottish, and German. The blond hair was another clue but not a Polish blond.

A guest on Fox's *Stossel*, the show created and hosted by television personality and author John Stossel was Paul Zak, a professor at Claremont Graduate University. Paul has the following very impressive credentials (from Wikipedia):

Paul J. Zak (born 9 February 1962) is an American neuroeconomist known as a proponent of neuroeconomics. His current work applies neuroscience to build high performance organizations and to understand and guide consumer decisions.

Zak graduated with degrees in mathematics and economics from San Diego State University before acquiring a PhD in Economics from the University of Pennsylvania. He is a professor at Claremont Graduate University in Southern California. He has studied brain imaging, and was the first to identify the role of oxytocin in mediating trusting behaviors between unacquainted humans.

There is more about him in Wikipedia or find his staff bio on the Claremont Graduate University website. My tip and Christmas present for the ladies, check out Paul Zak as he is so easy on the eyes. Professor Zak, is he Polish or not?

Found on EthniCelebs.com, Steve Carrell the star of television and film has a Polish mother. Add Steve to the long list of Polish ethnic comedians. He is probably most famous for his work in the television sitcom *The Office* along with John Krasinski and for the movie *Anchor Man* starring Will Ferrell.

Another Polish billionaire? Conrad Prebys, born into a blue-collar family from South Bend, Indiana, "joined the ranks of the world's billionaires" in 2015 (http://ceoworld.biz/2015/04/16/san-diego-based-real-estate-tycoon-conrad-t-prebys-is-now-a-billionaire). Conrad has the German given name, but his surname looks Eastern European. Conrad "Przebyszewski" Prebys, Polish or not?

More Polish names!! Received a genuinely nice eMail from Sue Czerwinski about her adorable grandson, Marek Czerwinski. Said babcia about her cutie:

Marek's name is the Polish version of "Mark" and means "warlike" although this little fellow is more about happiness and peace than war. Already 2 years of age, Marek has already enjoyed pierogis and other Polish traditional foods. Marek loves airplanes, trains, his books and playing with his dog, Sneakers.

March 2016

A Polish Pro-lifer

Spring. Easter. For Christians, it is the time of Resurrection and new life. Life. Are you for or against life?

Usually the thinking around the sanctity of life begins and centers on abortion. I prefer the comprehensive approach that the Catholic Church espouses, from cradle to grave and everything in between. Two people said things that I think are interesting perspectives on the right to life and especially on the "in between" part.

I have heard a lot of stirring homilies over the years but the one I heard Pro-life Sunday this past January brought me, and brought most everyone at Mass to tears. As proof, turning around for the hand-shake of peace I was surprised to find that the two girls sitting behind me were still teary-eyed and sobbing. Instead of beating us over the head abortion is bad, Father Dan asked all of us to consider the underlying meaning for the act of abortion which is the surrender to contraception, not only of the physical, of pills for instance, but the contraception that is a state of mind. The definition of contraception uses the words inhibit, prevent, or restrict and this affects the smallest child all the way up to the most rugged man. The denouement of the sermon was his personal story of intervention and how much he loves receiving "grace" in his life, but also Grace, in the form of a bubbly and beautiful little girl.

The other reference that had a good "everything in between" sentiment was a speech by the Republican candidate Carley Fiorina. She spoke of her early experience in the business world and how at one point she was told to "settle" into a position and go along with the status quo. She explained how happy she was to have never "settled" for things she thought could be improved or for outcomes that could be better. Whatever your opinion about Carley, I think it is safe to say she has a fire in her belly for life and what it has to offer.

There are countless examples of Poles that embraced life in all of its fullness, became successful, and made any number of contributions to humanity, including in the realm of Pro-life. Recently I finished reading the excellent book, *The Auschwitz Volunteer: Beyond Bravery, Captain Witold Pilecki, Prisoner No. 4859* (Aquila Polonica, 2012). Some might think it strange to use a concentration camp experience as an example for Pro-life but I think this comparison to the abortion industry is real and fits.

Just as the fences around Auschwitz blocked all civil normalcy and German Nazism was contraception to all the life outside of the sphere of Hitler's terrible cult, the "halflings" (camp inmates and prisoners) were like feint heartbeats inhabiting the inner sanctum of that awful place of death. Not knowing what lied before him, Pilecki volunteered to be captured and sent to Auschwitz to report to the Polish government and the allies what was going on in the camp. The book is his diary of his incarceration inside the camp and it is obvious he was engaged fully in completing the mission. The following excerpt confirms this as Captain Pilecki reflects on the reaction of new captures from Warsaw (page 242):

My comrades whom I have mentioned and who had come in from Warsaw… remarked that they had not expected to find the inmates' physical condition and morale in Auschwitz to be so good. They said they had known nothing about the brutality here, the "wall of tears," nor about the phenol or the gas chambers.

They themselves had not thought, and no one in Warsaw had seriously considered that Auschwitz could represent an active asset; for the most part people felt that everyone there was a skeleton whom it was pointless and useless to rescue.

It was bitter listening to this while looking at the lads' brave faces.

Witold Pilecki was fighting not only for his life but the life of his comrades, and the life of the nation. By staying alive he was fighting for life in general. So many of us Poles give in to the contraception of our self-respect and dignity and accept restrictions and inhibitions imposed upon us by society and the greater world in which we live.

Pro-life is about birth, family, language, culture, death, and the remembrance and the history of all of them. Cradle to grave and all that is in between. Captain Pilecki rejected the forces of contraception in his world and he certainly did not settle in accepting it. Should we?

Polish Babes and Babies

Wow!! (Polish translation: "Wow!!") Lindsay Czarniak born in Harrisburg, Pennsylvania November 7, 1977 has been employed in several television sports related programs including reporting on the 2008 Summer Olympics, NASCAR Sprint Cup Series, and as a host on ESPN's SportsCenter. Beautiful Polish name and beautiful lady but Lindsay, Polish or not?

On a roll for another Polish named baby. Kamil and Celeste Kuczewski have a new baby, Boleslaw Kamil Kuczewski, better known as "Bolek." Bolek is three months old and is, as I have been hearing a lot lately, too cute! Congratulations to the Kuczewski's and their beautiful little boy.

April 2016

Poland Charting

*F*irst things, Frank Nice, the humanitarian and author featured in the February Pondering Pole has another son, Frank III, who prefers to go by the Polish nickname "Franus." Pokorne przeprosiny (humble apologies) Franus for neglecting to mention you in that column but I will not forget to say now, great name!!

Often I mention the Yahoo "ticker." For those of you not familiar, if you go to the yahoo.com main page, there are links to mail, sports, finance, and other popular searches and there are also streams of article posts about a number of topics (politics, entertainment, sports, and general news) from a variety of public sources. Those info threads showing only the title, short description, and a small picture, are what I call the Yahoo ticker. Like the telegraphic stock tickers of the past, information is listed down the page in a continuous stream.

Love the ticker and lately I am confused, astounded, and happy. What little news is reported about Poland at all is usually negative and now I am seeing blips on the ticker, almost every day, with some good, some bad, but overall, only regular news about Poland. Check it out yourself and here are some examples from my personal "Poland Charting" during the month by title, authors, and sources.

Tusk, Duda not Poles apart on EU problem of law changes by Raf Casert for the Associated Press.

Polish Prime Minister: No Risk of EU Sanctions Against Poland by Monika Scislowska for the Associated Press.

Poland upgrading Leopard Tanks in response to new Russian Armata Tanks.

Constitutional Crisis Veers Poland Into Uncharted Territory by Andrew Macdowall.

They are predominantly political posts coming from the Associated Press but the person or group responsible for the posts on the "ticker" has a very keen interest in what is going on in Poland. Does anyone know who our Yahoo friend is or how to find out who it is?

One of those unknown friends posted an article that made me especially astounded and happy. The title of the article from *Foreign Policy* magazine is *The Moral Perils of Being Polish* by Emily Tamkin (https://foreignpolicy.com/2016/02/29/the-moral-perils-of-being-polish-lech-walesa-communist-informant-solidarity). Her first line of the piece is "Lech Walesa, Poland's legendary dissident, may have been a communist informant, but that makes him neither hero nor villain --- only complicated, like his country." Yes! It is complicated being Polish. If you have a real Polish name, there is the pronunciation thing; there is the negative perception thing; the joke thing; anti-Semitism thing; do I fight or do I compromise or do I just go along thing; do the Polish or do the American thing; and whatever is the next thing. Life is complicated for us Poles.

And life in Poland during the 70s and 80s was complicated for Walesa. The subject of this work is about the recently released documents indicating how the great leader of the Solidarity movement that gained Poland freedom from the Soviet Union and catapulted Eastern Europe into an independence and freedom frenzy might have colluded with the communist government from 1970 to 1976. Seems impossible to believe but at the least the charge skews the image we have of Walesa as just a simple hard-working man turned hero.

As Niccolo Machiavelli said in *The Prince*: "There is none so disadvantaged as he that will attempt to bring about change. For, by definition, he has many powerful enemies and but few weak friends." Walesa was trying to wrestle a minute amount of change from the grip of the "Evil Empire." Whether he had a strategy, was confused, or really was acting as a double agent, all that seems irrelevant when we think about the outcome at the Lenin Shipyards. Ms. Tamkin explains it this way:

These documents exist in the first place not despite Walesa's long-standing opposition to communist rule, but because of it. Those who were politically active — as Walesa was even in the 1970s — were more likely to be kept under surveillance, persecuted, and pressured to inform on fellow opposition activists than those who lived quiet lives according to communist strictures.

That is a deeply insightful possible perspective on Lech Walesa's behavior before and during Solidarity and certainly is not an explanation that can be understood in simple black or white terms. She goes on to say,

The people and politicians of Poland lived through persecution, suppression, resistance, and transition. All of that has been brought into its civic life today. There are no angels and villains in civil society in Poland, because there are no such people anywhere, and particularly not in countries that have lived under political persecution and have gone through such intense periods of transition. The Polish people can't afford to avoid reckoning with that truth, for even as the remaining public figures that lived under communism grow old and pass away and are replaced by those who merely remember them, their complicated personal histories are necessarily going to be a part of Poland's political future.

I am not familiar with Emily Tamkin but her beautiful summation of the current political situation in Poland and really the life and history of the Polish people is priceless. She is right, Poland time and again had to confront and deal with complicated circumstances to survive. We can examine and debate the context and motives to judge the true nature of the personalities and events we read about. History is replete with surprises and more and more we are learning that historical figures have back stories that sometimes shock and disappoint us. Sorting through all of it can be complicated, but it is also enlightening and rewarding.

Polish or Not?

My Polish life just keeps getting better and better. Heidi Przybyla is a contributing political analyst on the Fox News channel. Beautiful, smart, Slavic looking, and flashing a killer Polish name, Polish or not?

Mike Souchak, PGA golfer during the 50s and 60s, who won 15 times on the tour, Polish or not? Mike was good enough to beat Palmer and Nicolaus in his career. That, is special.

Terry James "TJ" Lubinsky, radio personality and more important, "executive producer/director of many Public Broadcasting Service (PBS) pledge-drive programs. He presents oldies-format music programs airing on PBS." Polish or not? How about a TJ wanna-be film for some of the old great polka stars playing a set of their finest hits? "We have operators ready to take your pledges… "

June 2016

The Chico Marx Effect

*I*t is estimated that only 10% of the Mayan civilization has been uncovered on the Yucatan peninsula. In a similar study, only 20% of the most famous and important people in the world that are Polish have been identified. Okay, that last one I made up.

I was given a special assignment to research how Italians felt about the character "Chico" (played by Leonard Marx) of the Marx Brothers comedy troupe, most popular in the 1930s in comedies like *Duck Soup, Animal Crackers,* and *A Night at the Opera.* While all of the brothers were wacky and clownish, their "shtick" was that they were a bunch of smarty-pants using funny digs and wise cracks to put down or show up or discombobulate the people and circumstances around them. They also portrayed a certain demographic with Groucho as the nutty professor, Harpo the hyperactive child that only music can tame, and Chico, "Chiccolini," the dimwitted (according to some sources) Italian immigrant.

Most of the internet searches I conducted did not turn up much. There is though, an interesting 2009 blog called *Toonzone* (http://www.toonzone.net/ the-chico-marx-effect/) in which the author, Ed Liu, an Asian American, talks about the "The Chico Marx Effect." Here is Ed's definition of what it is.

I love Chico Marx.

I love Chico Marx, despite the fact that fundamentally, he's a non-Italian guy affecting an accent to depict ethnic people for the entertainment of other white people.

I call this "The Chico Marx Effect," and it's something that drives me nuts: I want to find an intellectually honest explanation that lets me continue to hate Charlie Chan and love Chico Marx, even though they're both doing the exact same thing… Why is Chico Marx funny,

but Rob Schneider faking a thick Asian accent for that Chuck and Larry movie isn't?

Ed Liu is saying depicting ethnic people in stereotypical, silly, or even demeaning ways is okay as long it is not your ethnic group. He also might as well be saying it is human nature to be okay when your neighbor's ox is gored… but not yours.

It will take a lot more research to find out what percentage of Italians accept or reject the Chico character, but it really doesn't matter what they thought of Chico in 1935. For the record, I have one Italian buddy who "hates" *The Godfather* and another who told me he was embarrassed seeing *Saturday Night Fever*. At this point, it is easy to extrapolate from the anecdotal data that most Italians are finished with the Chicos, the Chinese are finished with Charlie Chan, and the Polish are finished with Sophie Kuchinsky of *Two Broke Girls*, among others. Among many others. Let me take this a couple steps farther and expand on the Chico Effect.

The next part is "there is always someone worse off than you" syndrome. They might be picking on us but hey, there were groups before us that got picked on, some much worse. Finally, there is the "Do we always have to be politically correct?" What's the matter with Jennifer Coolidge playing Sophie Kuchinsky? Kowalski, lighten up wood ja! All three of these are standard human reactions, we've all been there, and the truth is they are based on a need to divert attention from personal inadequacies or disadvantages and to feel good or feel part of the larger community.

So how do we deal with The Chico Marx Effect now?

If the ethnic character that is not Polish is shown in a poor light and if you feel any sense of respect for your own ethnicity, it can't be funny. Resist piling on.

Just because someone or somebody is suffering or has suffered does not mean you should endure insults and derision. There are no evens-stevens in abuse. Don't tell me how the Irish were made fun of in the 1840's and now it's our turn. We want to celebrate the best in everyone.

When you hear someone say, "well, I guess I have to be politically correct," the right response is, "no, you just have to be correct." 99% of the time what a person does or says reluctantly, "to be politically correct," simply means they need to adjust their perspective. Saying "Redskins" or "colored" or "Oriental" is not racist or necessarily insensitive, however, they are not preferred and they certainly are not respectful, prevalent, or nice. Being correct is the new nice.

Polish Popeye or Not?

In the book, *Popeye, An Illustrated History of E.C.Segar's Character in Print, Radio, Television and Film Appearances, 1929-1993*, by Fred Grandinetti (McFarland & Company, Inc., 1994), there is the history of what is believed to be the basis for the character we know as Popeye. That inspiration was a Polish man from Segar's hometown of Chester, Illinois named Frank "Rocky" Fiegel.

The first appearance of Popeye as we know him, the "odd-looking, fat-fore-armed, pipe-smoking sailor" began in 1929 but his development was born January 27, 1868. Frank Fiegel lived, worked, and fought his tormentors in Chester, Illinois. As Grandinetti tells it:

The lore of Chester, Illinois, holds that the character of Popeye was inspired by town resident Frank "Rocky" Fiegel. Lee Huffstutler, herself a Chester local, makes and well supports this argument. According to Huffstutler, Rocky Fiegel was of Polish descent and lived with his mother in a house near the Evergreen Cemetery. Mrs. Huffstutler describes him as "tall, strong, always ready for a fight and always a winner."

The web site findagrave.com, shows his parents as being born in Poland. The story about this man and his life actually is a little sad. I am wondering if the mumbling that Popeye is noted for is mumbling that Fiegel did because he was an English-as-a-second-language person.

I will confess and ask forgiveness when I was part of a cabal of rascals that made fun of a man that mumbled his speech and conversation. When my mom heard the mocking, she informed me that the mumbler, also a Polish man, did not speak English until he was eight years old. That story matched with Popeye's quirky feature and struck a nerve. Forgive me Dear Lord.

Polish or Not?

I cannot remember how I found Luisa Omielan, a British comedian "born in Birmingham to parents of Polish descent." Luisa is famous now for her "thigh gap" routine that went viral and amassed over 30 million views on Facebook. Her stuff is adult in nature so be forewarned but she presents well. You can judge the comedy level.

"Working for the Weekend" is the hit we hear on the radio often and it was the work of 80s rock band Loverboy. Mike Reno and Paul Dean are the leaders (the band is still doing gigs and Mike is still sporting the headband). Mike was born Joseph Michael Rynoski. Ethnicelebs shows his father as Polish (http://ethnicelebs.com/mike-reno). Chalk up another Polish rocker.

July 2016

"Let democracy work in Poland."

*P*avelski, Kesolowski, Gronkowski, Lewandowski, and Krzyzewski. It is so much fun following sports these days with so many prominent "skis."

And dzia dzia just spent four days with grandson Lucca Stanislaus. He is simply amazing and getting cuter all the time. I hope you have or will have a little Stanislaus or Stanislawa in your family.

Sports and grandbabies are beautiful and benign distractions. Now on to the real world and the topic in recent months is the constitutional "upheaval" in Poland. Like politics everywhere, getting a handle on what is really happening is hard to decipher but it is also what makes it so interesting. In Poland, it seems to be all about the constitution, what is constitutional, and who adheres more to it. Sound familiar?

If you are not up on the background and details of the criticism directed at the new Law and Justice Party (PiS) government, there is a summary of the history and platform of PiS in Wikipedia. There are also two perspectives that are hundreds of years apart but seem to be very similar in tenor and approach as it pertains to the Polish character and to the constitutional government they embraced in the late 1700s and after independence in the 1980s.

The French philosopher and political commentator Jean-Jacques Rousseau gave his opinion on forming the Polish constitution of 1772 in his dissertation "Considerations on the Government of Poland and on Its Proposed Reformation." Rousseau's blueprint for what was happening during the transition period right before the partitions are eerily prophetic of what is happening now with the new Polish government. I strongly encourage you to read it. His understanding of the Polish people and the meddling of Poland's neighbors could be from a page in a 2016 article from a google search on the internet. Rousseau says,

Incline the passions of the Poles in a different direction, and you will give their souls a national physiognomy which will distinguish them from other peoples, which will prevent them from mixing, from feeling at ease with those peoples, from allying themselves with them; you will give them a vigor which will supplant the abusive operation of vain precepts, and which will make them do through preference and passion that which is never done sufficiently well when done only for duty or interest.

… Loving the fatherland, they will serve it zealously and with all their hearts. Given this sentiment alone, legislation, even if it were bad, would make good citizens; and it is always good citizens alone that constitute the power and prosperity of the state.

There is equal vigor with the victor and the vanquished if we are to believe the numbers of supporters and protestors in Poland. The true solution remains to be seen and like all nations, the swing from liberal to conservative or some combination is typical of the democratic process. Remember Margaret Thatcher? Remember Sarkozy? There is complaining in this country that China or India are competing and gaining a greater share in the world market but it was the United States that promoted this economic model. So Poland is acting like a Western country; so be it.

Still, if the constant barrage of news about PiS is a little disconcerting then the words of Edmund Janniger, a special representative of the Minister of National Defense of the Republic of Poland may help to calm and dampen the hysteria. In an article from the NewsMax World website "Overreach in Poland Leads to New Justice Appointments" (http://www.newsmax.com/World/GlobalTalk/poland-judicial-court/2016/06/02/id/731898/), he explains the situation in mater-of-fact terms that basically says, anything that is happening in our country has been done in yours. He writes:

Most recently, President Obama has seen his nomination of a new U.S. Supreme Court Justice in the last year of his administration widely resisted by Congress on the grounds that the winner of the upcoming presidential election should make that choice, since it will affect the balance of power on America's highest constitutional tribunal.

Observers can agree or disagree with how the American political process ultimately handled these matters relating to the distribution of power between the branches of government in the U.S., but we should all agree that they were and are internal matters that are the business of the American people... They are decidedly none of Europe's business, and certainly none of the business of international bodies.

I have to admit I don't understand the intense interest from the European community on how Poland governs herself, at least in this early stage of the process. Janniger is calling for patience and tolerance and to give President Duda and his cabinet a chance. We heard this same sentiment over and over again concerning President Obama.

One of the big complaints expressed in the United States is that our Congress is not getting anything done. Democracy is a preferred philosophy but on a practical level it is very, very inefficient and moves slow. We would all like to make our friends say and believe what we do but that is not how it works. If you want to get a lot done, get a dictatorship. Janniger, as well as Rousseau, give the Poles a lot more credit than many of the experts.

Poland should be judged by the international community on how it relates to mutual security concerns and economic stability in Europe. On both of these important counts the new government in Poland has proven to be a reliable partner to NATO and the EU.

... If helping keep Europe free and prosperous are the touchstones by which Poland's government is fairly measured, the current Law and Justice government is off to a strong start.

The Polish people have proven the experts wrong before and I am sure this is another one of those instances.

August 2016

When Traveling Through St. Louis This Summer

*I*f you are passing through or scheduling a stop in the Mound City this August or even into the Fall season, here is a list of the churches in the area. Even if you do not belong to these religions, I recommend these places for the Polish cultural or historical tourist.

St. Stanislaus Kostka Church (http://www.saintstan.org/index.html). This is the historical Mother Church of the Poles in St. Louis and it is an example of a beautifully designed and restored place of worship. It truly is one of the gems on the list of historical churches in the city. St. Stans is no longer a Roman Catholic parish though. Please note from the website:

We proudly profess Catholic faith and celebrate Catholic sacraments, but we are no longer a part of the Archdiocese of St. Louis, nor do we belong to the institutional Roman Catholic Church.

St. Agatha Catholic Church (http://www.polishchurchstlouis.org/). St. Agatha is a Roman Catholic parish with a congregation and Mass in the Polish language. It is just down the street from the Anheuser-Busch brewery and the church and neighborhood are wonderful.

Polish National Catholic Church of Metropolitan St. Louis (http://stlpncc.org/page_1.htm). There is a PNC church community in St. Louis and there is another on the Illinois side of the Mississippi. Consult the web site for more information.

Black Madonna Shrine, Eureka, Missouri (http://www.franciscancaring.org/blackmadonnashri.html). This shrine designed and built by Polish Franciscan Brother Bronislaus Luszcz, is a beautiful meditative place "set in a countryside atmosphere that refreshes the body and soul." The Mass schedule is irregular so check first for that.

If traveling through Chicago...

But if you decide to skip St. Louis and visit the "Second City," be sure to see St. John Cantius chosen as "America's Most Beautiful Church" (http://www. chicagotribune.com/news/local/breaking/ct-st-cantius-church-award-met-2-20160419-story.html). I have not been there but this church, in the Goose Island neighborhood and built by Polish immigrants, won the "Church Madness" contest begun by Patrick Murray, "a self-proclaimed liturgy geek and consultant for Granda Liturgical Arts, a church design company in Omaha, Nebraska." I have seen an online slideshow of St. John's and it truly is amazing.

Please note there is talk of tearing the church down even after an anonymous benefactor pledged one million dollars to help renovate it. I get the fact that we have a lot of old, hard-to-maintain urban churches, but I just cry thinking about losing another beautiful, majestic historical structure, especially one that has a Polish imprint on it. Pray the Chicago Archdiocese allows this place to go on.

Naming Up North

Upon visiting the College of St. Benedict this summer (https://www.csbsju. edu/about/college-of-saint-benedict) located in St. Joseph, Minnesota, you will find the Gorecki Center, a "beautiful dining and conference center that offers state-of-the-art technology and consists of six meeting rooms that can accommodate large general sessions with seating for up to 500 people or smaller breakout rooms. The center was designed with two lobbies, a fireplace, an outdoor patio area, and windows from every view." There is the Kennedy Center and now the Gorecki Center. This is an example of great signage and remember if you want to infuse a Polish presence into the American mosaic, pay for a park bench or donate the funds for a university building. You will be creating a legacy and it is a perfect way to really teach the students about diversity.

Polish or not?

A while back I asked if Chicago-born and accordion-playing Dennis De Young of the rock group Styx was Polish. He is not. However, one of the earliest members of the band was John "J.C." Curulewski. Like De Young and the rest of the guys in the band, J.C. was a Chicago native.

While De Young was the driving force and genius behind Styx's early success and later along with Tommy Shaw propelled them to super star status, J.C., a solid performer and rocker played acoustic and electric guitar and wrote a number of the songs on the first five studio albums the band produced. What struck me most reading about him was his humanity and giving nature.

He left the band right when it was ready to bust out to be with his family, coach his son's baseball team, give guitar lessons, and eventually teach and mentor some of Chicago's best young guitar players. Too good a person apparently to die so young of a brain aneurysm at age 38. John Curulewski, Polish or not?

Joanna Hoffman, marketing executive and contemporary of Apple's Steve Jobs. She was one of the original members of the Apple Computer MacKintosh team and the NeXT team. Joanna was born in Poland, the daughter of Polish director Jerzy Hoffman and his Armenian former wife Marlene. Check out Kate Winslett's Polish accent playing Hoffman in the motion picture *Jobs*. Not bad.

Julie Pace, Associated Press correspondent and frequent commentator on *Fox News Sunday* with Chris Wallace, born in Buffalo, New York. Is Julie, Polish or Not?

September 2016

California (and Polish) Dream'n.

Ah Los Angeles. Drink it in. As Ron Burgundy would say, "stay classy." Stay classy, you Polonians.

Los Angeles is a collection of "type" communities and municipalities. For instance, Glendale, California is historically the Armenian area and on my recent trip there were many Kardashian look-a-like sightings. There is China Town, Korea Town, Hispanic barrios, West Hollywood, and many others. There aren't any current or historic neighborhoods (that I know of) for the Poles but there are two places you might want to visit on your next trip to LA to satisfy your Polish fix. One is Our Lady of the Bright Mount Church and the other is the "Polka" Polish restaurant. You can find directions and information on the web for both.

The Bright Mount Church is a spiritual and social gathering place for Polish Roman Catholics in Los Angeles. Legend has it that the property was owned and later donated by the famous Polish silent movie actress Barbara Apollonia Chalupiec, aka, Pola Negri. The truth is the land was purchased for a "ridiculously low price" from the Doheny oil family by the Polish community of Los Angeles in the 1940s and later incorporated as a Roman Catholic parish into the Los Angeles diocese.

Pola was a member of the parish for many years, gave generously to the building of the church, and according to one current member, bought and donated the Stations of the Cross that are on the walls to this day. My wife Sue commented on how beautiful they were before we learned of Pani Negri's connection to them.

The church is modern and beautiful and the grounds are amazing. The Polish congregation has done a superb job of adding to and improving the property. Like most Catholic churches, and especially with Polish churches, the parish is a religious as well as a cultural center for the congregation. For instance, the weekend of our visit, Our Lady of the Bright Mount had a commemoration program for veterans of World War II. Enjoyed meeting Andrzej Stefanski, 92 years young, although having the energy of a 52 year old. And a side note, the Polish faces are the same but the digs and garb are California style'n.

Need pierogi? The Polka Polish restaurant serves all the Polish standards but presents them very well and in ample portions. Dinners are built around the big four, pierogi, cabbage rolls, kielbasa, and bigos, and they also serve a Polish style of gulasz which is very reminiscent of my mom's roast beef and gravy. Absolutely delicious and thank you Polka for that. Hopefully they will have spinach soup the day you are there. Chicken, fish, and pork loin are also available. It is great neighborhood dining with a Polish flare. You will not be disappointed and for a reasonable price.

The Los Angeles adventure provided the opportunity to not only visit my daughter Brig and her husband Alex, but also to meet with two dear friends, Andy and Liz Kozlowski, who extended true Polish warmth and hospitality. They are super family people, mainstays of the Polish way, and oh, a lot of fun to be around! We had a blast.

Polish or not?

Marc Theissen is an American author, columnist, and political commentator. The former speechwriter for President George Bush the younger, he is a frequent guest on Fox News *The Kelley File*. Thiessen grew up on the Upper East Side in Manhattan, where both his parents were doctors and "left-of-center liberal Democrat types." His mother grew up in Poland and fought as a teenager in the Warsaw Uprising in which his grandfather died.

Mike Foltynewicz is a pitcher for the Atlanta Braves major league baseball team. The name is obviously Polish, and in this case, surprisingly, so was the pronunciation. Instead of the standard fowl-tin'-a-witz, the announcers pronounced his name in the Polish way, fool-ti-nay'-vich (accent on the next-to-last syllable). Hearing that name pronounced so fluidly and easily begs the question, why on earth did our people ever think that changing or phoneticizing Polish names was needed? You go Mike!!! You go the parents of Mike!!

October 2016

Something There is That Doesn't Love a Wall

"Before I built a wall I'd ask to know what I was walling in or walling out…"

— Robert Frost, *Mending Wall*

We are hearing a lot of talk about a wall this political season, those who want one and those who are not sure what they are walling out. There are physical and psychological walls, restrictions, barriers, and people who say no to everything. Whatever the circumstance, the wall concept is prevalent in many places and forms.

A famous restauranteur in St. Louis and big time ethnic guy told me that at his church, "the ladies in the kitchen just don't let just anybody in there but they let me help." Very hilarious if you knew the man and the situation but my own ethnic experience has shown time and again how "guarding" the kitchen or the church or the club or the choir seems to be universal among the immigrants.

Part of it most likely comes from protecting oneself from hostile elements both from within and outside the community. It is about securing and guarding the turf. Some of it comes from tribal tradition and who is anointed to participate in the event or ceremony. Some is just pure competition. When you have struggled so hard to "build" or attain anything, protectiveness seems to be a natural progression and trait.

Poland, as we know, has had a lot of experience with invaders, walls, and barbed-wire fences. Portions of the ancient wall around the old city of Krakow still exist and it is a reminder of the time when the Poles had to defend that beautiful city. Compare these walled fortifications though to Krakow's city square, which is rated by Touropia as one of the "14 Famous City Squares Around the World" (http://www.touropia.com/city-squares-around-the-world/). Keep in mind the list includes Trafalgar in London, Tianamen in Beijing, Saint Peter's in Rome, and Red Square in Moscow.

A popular tourist attraction in Poland, the Main Market Square (Rynek Główny) in the Old Town in Kraków is the largest medieval town square in Europe dating back to the 13th century. The square is surrounded by historical townhouses, historic buildings, palaces and churches. The center of the square is dominated by the Cloth Hall, rebuilt in 1555 in the Renaissance style, topped by a beautiful attic. Rising above the city square are the Gothic towers of Saint Mary's Basilica.

Consider the town square. Squares are the opposite of walls; they are open, welcoming, and bustling with activity. There is no better time to groom the second in command, teach the young kids, and introduce the traditions to those new to or outside the group. Maybe some of it will actually stick and something good will come about in fresh and exciting ways. It is never a bad idea to rethink what we "are walling in and what we are walling out."

On a sad note, we buried my uncle James "Jimmy" Lamczyk September 3rd, 2016. He was a farmer by trade but looking at the pictures of his life at the funeral home, he was part Steve McQueen, part Saint John Paul II, and full-time, all-around happy family man. I have mentioned men and women that I thought were stellar and complete human beings and here was another shining example. He married the perfect partner and friend, Brenda Kiselewski, he was the father of four kids, eleven grandchildren, and ten great grandchildren. That I could see there were no walls around this guy. Life extended from a run on the beach to four-wheeling with a grandchild around the farm. Na Zdrowie! and God bless you Jimmy Lamczyk. You will be missed.

Polish or Not?

James Rado, born James Alexander Radomski is a member of The Songwriters Hall of Fame (http://songwritershalloffame.com), and is "an American actor, playwright, director, and composer. Rado is best known as the co-author, along with Gerome Ragni, of 1967's groundbreaking American tribal love-rock musical *Hair*. He and Ragni were nominated for the 1969 Tony Award for best musical, and they won for best musical at the Grammy Awards in 1969." As his bio in the Hall of Fame explains:

In 1967, jazz critic and music publisher Nat Shapiro introduced Galt Mac Dermot to Gerome Ragni and Jim Rado, actors who had just written a provocative play entitled Hair. The three hit it off, and Mac Dermot scored the music to Ragni and Rado's words in three weeks. It was a match made in songwriting heaven.

Rado has said that the inspiration for the music came from a combination of people they met in the street, people they knew and their own imaginations. Hair won a Grammy in 1969 and was made into a hit film in 1979. The theatrical show ran for nearly 2000 performances in both London and New York.

A couple of the most famous hits co-written by him are "Aquarius" and "Let the Sunshine In." James "Radomski" Rado, Polish or not?

Sonia Rykiel, the "Queen of Knitwear," dead at age 86. Most of the biographical information shows her father as a watchmaker from Romania and her mother Russian. The *Jewish Telegraph Agency* news site reports that the "Paris native was the daughter of a Polish Jewish mother" (http://www.jta.org/2016/08/25/news-opinion/sonia-rykiel-queen-of-knitwear-fashion-designer-dies-at-86). Sonia Rykiel, Polish or Russian?

Keith Urban, mega-super Country Western star, and host during the final seasons of *American Idol*, is he Polish or German? I would encourage you to read the discussion on a website called Geni and in particular a discussion in the Geni Polska Profile section about the ancestral roots of Keith's surname, Urban (https://www.geni.com/discussions/131133). Is it Urbahn or Urbanski? As I read it, the argument and evidence are very convincing for Polish.

The Olympics have concluded but there is one more bronze for the Poles. To the question, which country has the best computer programmers? (http://www.cnet.com/news/which-country-has-the-best-programmers-hint-its-not-the-us/), according to HackerRank, "a company that focuses on competitive programming challenges for both consumers and businesses," it is China first, with Russia second, and Poland third. The combined population of China and Russia is over 2 billion so grabbing the third spot is impressive. Congrats to all the Polish bombas!!

November 2016

Count The Fingers and Toes

When the baby is born, inevitably someone asks, "Got all the fingers and toes?"

The great, great majority of us are born whole, physically and mentally. Unfortunately a slight percentage will have some debilitating condition. In most cases though, even people with the most severe disabilities settle into life and are generally content. They are satisfied to do whatever they can. I often think of what it would be like to be blind, or paralyzed, or missing one or more limbs. The other day a person with a lifelong mental illness including bouts of living with pure hell, conceded he was happy with his life. I was surprised to hear him say that considering all he had endured.

Here is a story that is a little dated so if you have heard about Natalia Partyka then hopefully it will remind you about making the best of what you were given. Natalia, born in Poland, came into the world without a right hand and forearm but became a world class table tennis player. To be honest, playing table tennis, or as it is known in South Saint Louis, ping-pong, does not really require a person to have both hands and arms. One will suffice for the actual play and the other is mainly used in balancing the beer can. The great ones however, need two.

She most likely would have stayed entirely with para-competitions but her prowess in the sport made her gravitate toward competing in many whole-bodied competitions. Her most recent accomplishment was to make it to the round of 32 in the 2012 London Olympics. Before that "Partyka competed for Poland both in the 2008 Summer Olympics and the 2008 Summer Paralympics in Beijing – one of only two athletes to do so, the other being Natalie du Toit in swimming."

Her list of accomplishments in table tennis is quite extensive as she has won all of the colors of the medals possible. Besides her athletic success, Natalia has received the Knights Cross of the Order of Polonia Restituta (5th class) in 2008 and the Officer's Cross of the Order of Polonia Restituta (4th class) in 2013. She is an example for her country and the world.

While I am thankful and inspired by Natalia Partyka, as often happens, I get inspiration also from William Donohue, the President of the Catholic League for Religious and Civil rights. In the June 2016 issue of *Catalyst,* the League's monthly newsletter and "From the President's Desk," Dr. Donohue talks about the criticism leveled at the Catholic League for being "too tough and too pugnacious" in defense of the Church. Interesting and based on my anecdotal experience, true. When I mention the Catholic League to even devote Catholics, some tune me out because they feel the League is overbearing and wrong to stand up or answer back.

Too tough and too pugnacious or rather "responsible aggression" as Doctor Donohue prefers to describe it. Christianity teaches us to turn the other cheek, but on the other hand I would point to the story of Christ throwing the money lenders out of the temple not pugnacious or angry but responsible aggression. Donohue explains:

I have often said that the Catholic League is responsibly aggressive: we are responsible because we are Catholic; we are aggressive because we are a civil rights organization. To be sure, there is a certain degree of tension built into that formula, but it can be negotiated. No matter, what should never be discounted is the resolve of our adversaries – they come to win.

This is a phrase that Polonia can use and does use. In May of this year, former President Clinton said the countries of Poland and Hungary do not want "democracy." I don't think the response from both of those nations was over blown for calling him out; I think it could be characterized as responsible and aggressive.

We are civil rights people for ourselves and for others. We are not out to win anything in particular but we do espouse respectful acknowledgement, sincere recognition, and fair treatment. The next time someone says to you, don't get mad or I am sorry you are upset, you can reply, no, I was just being responsibly aggressive in responding to what you said!

Painting Czeslawa

One of the most iconic surviving photographs of the inmates of Auschwitz (and there were many of them), was an "identity" picture of a 14 year old Polish girl named Czeslawa Kwoka #26847. She was photographed by the chief camp photographer Wilhelm Brasse and her mug shot was a recording of between 40,000 and 50,000 inmate's individual photos. Czeslawa was "one of the 'approximately 230,000 children and young people aged less than eighteen' among the 1,300,000 people who were deported to Auschwitz-Birkenau from 1940 to 1945."

Painting Czeslawa Kwoka is a collaborative work by Theresa Edwards (who did the speaking part) and Lori Schreiner (who did the art work) of mixed media inspired by the three "identity" photographs of Czeslawa sometime in 1942 or 1943. It won the 2007 Tacenda Literary Award for Best Collaboration, presented by BleakHouse Publishing. Have you seen this painting and heard the poetry?

Polish or Not?

Wilhelm Brasse, Polish or not? Wilhelm's father was Austrian and his mother Polish. He was a professional photographer in Poland prior to World War II who was "known as the 'famous photographer of the Auschwitz concentration camp"; his life and work were the subject of the 2005 Polish television documentary film *The Portraitist (Portrecista),* which first aired in the "Proud to Present" series on the Polish TVP1 on 1 January 2006.

December 2016

Cultivating a "Cultural" Inheritance

Well, I guess the Poles on the Northside of Chicago got an early Christmas present!! Congratulations to the Cubbies, their fans, and their half-Polish manager Joe Maddon on winning the baseball World Series. (Mom Albina Klocek, "Beanie," is Polish and still works as a waitress at the Third Base Luncheonette in Hazelton, Pennsylvania.) Joe owes it all to a healthy diet of pierogis growing up!

We all know that Santa Claus is Polish because he wears red and white.

When I sit on Santa's lap this year, I will have two wishes. The first is that a very wealthy Polish person will take an active interest in our Polish-American people and become involved financially with a variety of institutions and organizations to help in their ability to function and continue their mission. Santa has most likely heard this wish many times in the past.

I'm surprised this hasn't happened already. For instance, where I went to high school, a family donated 25 million dollars for an arts center. One million to twenty five bona fide Polish causes or initiatives would go a long way. I'll even take one million to ten Polish causes. Which ones? Well, for starters the Kosciuszko Foundation, the Lira Ensemble, or The Polish American Journal have histories, accomplishments, and are current vital contributors to supporting and promoting Polonia. There are many others like them.

That wish ties in with the next wish. It was prompted in part by an article written by Don Eggleston, the System Vice President for Mission Integration for SSM Health, St. Louis, Missouri, titled "Cultivating an Inheritance." The word cultivate is very appropriate in this context and Don was talking about giving an inheritance that is not monetary but rather a part of someone or something that is meaningful and enriching in an emotional or psychological way to remember the giver. In the case of SSM Health, the thing passed is the "mission," the ministry of caring for and healing the sick and to "continue courageously for the love of God." He began with an example of how this happened in his family.

When my father was dying several years ago, he elected to give his children and grandchildren personal possessions by which we could remember him… I received my dad's shaving brush and mug and his shoeshine kit. I placed the brush and mug on top of the mirror in the bathroom, and I put the shoeshine kit to use when needed. When I shine my shoes, my dad certainly comes to mind.

To this day, I tend to order fish on Fridays. Remembering the "meatless Friday" obligation, also makes me think of Jesus Christ and my Christian faith. The shaving brush, shoeshine kit, and fish are valued references to people we love.

For the holiday season this year, do some cultivating of your own. Work the ground and plant a seed and give your kids or grandkids a gift that is a cultural inheritance of your Polish past. It might be the wedding picture of mom or dad or better yet, dzia dzia or babci on their wedding day.

Someone showed me a plaque of the beautiful Polish saying "Gosc w Dom, Bog w Dom" (a guest in the home is God in the home) handed down to him by his father. He has it hanging in his home. Pictures, plaques, an article of clothing, a costume, a dish, a prayer book, a CD of folk songs, a CD of favorite polka tunes, a book, whatever has a Polish mark on it that reminds them of who they are and where they came from. I suspect it will be worth more to them than another doll or toy dump truck or a candy cane from Santa.

Polish or Not?

Brad Goreski, originally from Canada and a dapper and handsome fellow is a fashion expert and co-host on the show *Fashion Police*. Even without Joan Rivers it is still fun to watch. Brad's father is Polish.

Chuck Zukowski is not insulted to be called a nut. You can read more about him at UFONUT.com. He is a UFO phenomenon investigator and is a proponent of the idea of the 37th Parallel theory which is a "highway" across America where most UFO sightings have been made. He has appeared in several UFO televised programs on the 37th Parallel and other topics. Chuck's name and face are Polish but is he, Polish or not?

Pola Negri is known as the Polish silent movie star but Theda Bara, real name Theodosia Burr Goodman, known as one of the first "sex symbols" of the silent film era, has a Polish connection as well. According to Wikipedia, her father "was a prosperous Jewish tailor born in Poland." While the silent female actresses all tend to look alike, Pola and Theda have an awfully close resemblance. Kissin' Polish cousins?

III

2017

Web Enabled

*I*n the first part of this story is a book review and in the second part, an update on a Polish American high tech entrepreneur. Both of them are web enabled.

Maybe you have seen the movie *My Dinner with Andre* with actors Wallace Shawn and Andre Gregory, or more recently, *Her*, starring Joaquin Phoenix, Amy Adams, and Scarlett Johansen. The stories are the interaction of people discussing intellectual, philosophical, or social topics. No cars blowing up in *My Dinner* and *Her*. The simple conversation between the principles and what they are thinking makes you think. That is also the premise in the book *Save Send Delete* by Danusha Goska (Roundfire Books, 2012).

Hopefully you know Danusha by her great opus, *Bieganski: The Brute Polak Stereotype, Its Role in Polish-Jewish Relations and American Popular Culture,* a book on anti-Polish defamation and bias that every Polish American, and every American for that matter, should read. *Save* takes on a different challenge, "is there a God in heaven?" and "is there love in human hearts?" Her approach though is the same as Bieganski: she is intensely inquisitive, analytical, and her support references are abundant and impressive.

In this story, she is the "poor Catholic schoolteacher" protagonist and holds her own as she debates a famous atheist celebrity by corresponding through e-mail. This is a story based on an experience from her life and the e-mail record is very creative and very contemporary. As one reviewer said, it is "a powerful and evocative reflective journey." I hope when you read *Save, Send Delete*, you experience that same journey.

Way back in 2010 an article was published on the Yahoo ticker "How to be a millionaire by age 25." One of the featured millionaires was Matt Mickiewicz.

Born in Kraków, Poland … Mickiewicz created his first website at the age of 14 called Webmaster-Resources.com, which later became Site-

Point. At 16, Mickiewicz traveled to Melbourne with his mother and met his soon to be business partner and co-founder, Mark Harbottle. At 16, Mickiewicz found himself closing $10,000 advertising deals between classes at high school. Mickiewicz barely finished high school and did not attend college.

Fast forward to 2016 and Matt is still in charge of his SitePoint enterprise and is doing quite well. The kid who didn't go to college is now worth 100 million according to celebritynetworth.com and is the "co-founder of the web companies Flippa, 99designs, and Hired." Matt is quoted as saying "Create massive value for others by providing a solution where no other exists." Good American business advice from the Krakow kid.

Polish or Not?

The migration of people. Samantha Morton, English actress, screenwriter, and director has a Polish connection on her mother's side. Back in the end of 2015, she joined the debate concerning which and how many refugees the British government should allow and how she has a personal, sort of, connection to it all.

"My grandparents were Polish refugees. I wouldn't be here if it wasn't for this country accepting my Polish grandparents." She added, "The world can change so quickly and if we are not careful this situation will become worse than the Second World War, it will be so horrific. I think in history people will look back and they will judge."

Samantha Morton, the granddaughter of Polish immigrants, "has been described as one of the greatest actors of her generation." Think about it.

And think about this. About the same time as I learned of Samantha Morton's "connection," I was watching the C-Span British parliament proceedings and one of the MPs stood up making a point about his parents being Italian immigrants and what was the Prime Minister Theresa May's position on immigration and the United Kingdom? I wondered if any British MPs were of Polish extraction.

There is at least one, Daniel Kawczynski, and while he is concerned about recent anti-Polish sentiments and actions in England, he spoke not only about Poles leaving Poland but Poles entering the United Kingdom and their impact on the economy (http://www.express.co.uk/news/politics/695805/Daniel-Kawczynski-Poland-immigration-Conservative-MP-Brexit-EU-referendum). Recently he said:

"Immigration is bad for Poland, because there are now cities and towns rapidly becoming depopulated in Poland and they're having real difficulties in providing essential public services as a result of this brain drain.

And it is bad for the United Kingdom where there are certain communities like Peterborough, and Boston, and Lincolnshire where local services are being overwhelmed by the sheer numbers."

The divergent positions of Morton and Kawczynski playing out across the North Sea are mirrored in the debates happening in Poland, the ancestral homeland. Of course, whenever there are two Poles in the room there will be two opinions.

Another from the Yahoo ticker's "How to be a millionaire by age 25" list in 2010 was Juliette Brindak, the Cofounder/CEO of "the all-girl tween and teen" social networking company, Miss O & Friends (MissOandFriends.com). In 2016, Miss O is going strong and Juliette's net worth according to thecelebritycafe.com is 30 million. Business Insider magazine quotes her as saying, "The goal for the site was, and still is, to help young girls build confidence and self-esteem." Noble cause and impressive young woman. Polish or Not?

February 2017

Good vs. Evil

*T*here is probably some data out there on what percentage of the human race is good and how much is evil. In the Old Testament, God destroyed Sodom and Gomorrah because ten righteous persons could not be found. If you are a Christian, you believe that evil exists in the world and it is the power of the Holy Spirit that confronts and ultimately defeats it. Evil exists but we also know there is the presence of good to counter it.

The presence or force for good; hopefully that is you and me. "You and me" in this case is those of us that trace our lineage back to that mystical place called Poland. No country or people have a perfect record or monopoly when it comes to war and oppression. Despite our good friend Jan Gross, the author of *Neighbors*, a book comparing the behavior of the Polish people to the Nazis in World War II, my feeling is that the Poles, on balance and throughout their history have, World War II included, been a force for good in their region, on the European continent, and beyond. There is not enough room for ten but how about four examples of "righteous" Poles.

If you have not seen the movie *The Infiltrator,* be warned that it is intense and action packed and you will need a strong stomach for the constant impending danger and violence. The film is based on a book by the same name written by Robert Mazur, an agent in the United States Customs Department. Infiltrator is a true story about Mazur's undercover work to identify and prosecute the money laundering operation and people sustaining the Columbian drug cartel lead by Pablo Escobar. In a very real way the case can be made that Robert Mazur, whose father's parents were born in Poland (the grandfather in Warsaw and the grandmother from Krakow), is a true American hero and made a major difference in the drug war. You can read more about him, the book, and the movie at http://www.robertmazur.com. Robert Mazur, a force for good.

Eugene F. Soltes, the Jakurski Family Associate Professor of Business Administration at the Harvard Business School was a guest on C-SPAN touting his new book, *Why They Do It: Inside the Mind of the White-Collar Criminal* (Perseus Books, LLC, 2016). Professor Soltes is very bright and articulate and I am eager to read his study on this subject. This "subject" is something that needs to be addressed. As a person who greatly values the role of business and economics in a free and market-based society, more interest and understanding on the ethics of creating, owning, managing, and leading an enterprise can't hurt. Much of the talk in our most recent election was about how the United States and other countries conduct their business. Eugene Soltes and *Why They Do It*, a force for good.

What also intrigued me was the "Jakurski Family" as the sponsor of the academic chair at such a prestigious place as the Harvard Business School. The history and background of the Jakurski family traces to Andre' Jakurski, an engineer and alumnus of the Harvard Business School. He was born and raised in Rio de Janeiro, Brazil, and is the son of Polish parents that fought and survived World War II.

As part of the Polish underground resistance during World War II, Andre' Jakurski's father forged documents to help those in danger change their identities. "My parents lost everything during the war," explains the family's only son, adding that his father carried luggage for a year at the Paris train station to save enough money to move to Brazil. "My father was an engineer, and my mother was an entrepreneur," says Jakurski, who, like his parents, has achieved remarkable success seizing business opportunities in Brazil.

Andre' gravitated toward the financial sector working for and owning banks in Brazil. In 1998 he went on to create JGP Asset Management and as of 2013 JGP manages an investment portfolio of $3.8 billion.

Jakurski and his wife Maria have given generously to various charities and educational institutions including Rio's British School, John's Hopkins University, and the Harvard Business School. He likes to keep quiet about the donating, and "gives quietly, if not anonymously." He has said, "We give to organizations that will have a multiplier effect." Andre' Jakurski is a fantastically talented and successful person. He is a force for good.

Her website (http://tatianamoroz.com) says she is a "singer, songwriter, and revolutionary" and when I saw this, I said, "Is that all?" Tatiana Moroz is all that and is the Polish (with some Ukrainian and Sicilian), spokesperson and prominent "female singer-songwriter in the Bitcoin" community. Bitcoin has been described as a payment system, digital currency, and electronic currency. My best attempt to summarize what Bitcoin does is saying it is another way to pay for stuff without access to a bank or credit card company.

Tatiana appeared on the Fox show *Stossel* to explain the value of Bitcoin especially in Third World countries where there is little monetary regulation and carrying currency actually can be dangerous. You can see the interview on YouTube and the example she gave was how women in Afghanistan have gained access and freedom by using this cyber currency. Tatiana Moroz: singer, songwriter, revolutionary, spokesperson for Bitcoin, and, a force for good.

Polish or Not?

Ken Peplowski plays a mean clarinet and "is sometimes compared to Benny Goodman in terms of tone and virtuosity." You are encouraged to see some of Ken's ability on YouTube. Quite a compliment to be compared to one of the kings of jazz and swing but maybe this is fitting since Benny Goodman's father came from Warsaw, Poland in 1892 and settled in Baltimore, Maryland. Kenny Peplowski from Cleveland, Ohio, Polish or Not?

Infant Holy, Infant Lowly (W Zlobie Lezy), is one of the most popular hymns in the Polish Kolendy collection. Not only am I hearing it sung more and more at non-Polish Catholic churches in St. Louis during Christmas, but this song was featured at the 2016 Christmas program at the Manchester United Methodist Church in Ballwin, Missouri.

Manchester's program employed a hundred-member choir, a bell ensemble, a twenty-piece orchestra, and a special guest soloist. It wasn't just a bunch of carolers from down the street. Most of the popular standards were performed and the arrangement and rendering of *Infant Holy, Infant Lowly* was beautiful. We truly have finally arrived in America.

March 2017

Come Home

As the Catholic Church goes so goes Polonia. In the February/March issue of *Catholic St. Louis* magazine, there was an article about how to "invite your family members back to church." Seeing the diminishing congregations at many of our churches I think most of us can relate to this especially with our kids, others in our family, and some in our social circle. Three of the author's approaches are to "be positive, avoid banter that is critical of some aspect of Church life," "be a good example, bring your faith into the world by the way you treat others," and "invite them to a dinner or other event at your parish."

Take out the word "Catholic" and insert Polish and here is a very relatable checklist for enticing a fellow Polish ethnic back to his or her ancestral roots. Let's compare. Would you join a club if you heard bad things about it or the members? Positive is big selling point and there is a lot in Polonia to be positive about. Be a good example. Your involvement, encouragement, and interest are traits noticed and hopefully emulated by others, especially young people. If you write off your Polishness, they will too.

Finally, and this is one that typically does it for me, invite them to a dinner or event. I can hear or read about something, even how great something is, but until I actually experience it, I will not be convinced. Not only am I Polish (we do not trust anybody), but I am from Missouri and you have to "show" me.

Do not be afraid to ask either. I am surprised at how many events I thought questionable, thinking the invitees would hate it only to find out how highly it was deemed by them later. It is a big mistake to anticipate a reaction or feeling in another instead of letting them decide. Give someone a "taste" of Poland and you might be surprised how much it is enjoyed and appreciated.

That said, here are two amazing Polish guys you could invite to the festival. Maybe they will invite you to the festival! Or maybe to the beach! Follow me on this.

If you saw the movie Pulp Fiction, that driving guitar riff at the beginning is from the song "Misirlou" written by "The King of the Surf Guitar," the great Dick Dale, born Richard Anthony Monsour. Dick's father and family are of Lebanese descent and his mother's family emigrated from Poland. His life and list of accomplishments are rich and extensive: he "pioneered the surf music style," "experimented with reverberation" (a guitar playing method), worked with inventor Leo Fender in the creation of a new amplifier, and was involved in the design of the Fender Stratocaster guitar.

Dale's musical ability includes performing on instruments such as the oud, the tarabaki, the ukulele, and he began playing the piano at age nine. His strongest musical influence came from the Middle-Eastern Lebanese side of the family and he was a great admirer of Hank Williams. He started surfing when he was 17, beat rectal cancer in his thirties, wrote songs, recorded albums, and was a consummate performer even catching the attention of none-other-than Jimi Hendrix for his staccato picking, percussive, and heavy bending playing style.

What a giant of American culture! If you want to see what a burly Slavic looking guy looks like pounding a Fender Stratocastor, take a peek of Dick playing "Misirlou" on YouTube. Amazing and he is still going strong at age 78. You can search a number of sources on his life and work on the web.

From the Southern California surf scene we go next to Northern California and into the realm of an entirely different sound and culture and the music soul of San Francisco. Are you thinking Tony Bennett? If Tony is the "heart," then according to at least one writer, J.C. Juanis, the "Soundtrack of The City," the city being San Francisco, California, is from the mind and spirit of George Michalski.

George was born there but both of his parents were born in Poland and George's mom, now 97, still speaks in Polish. He was a musical prodigy, performing his first piano recital (a piece by Bach) when he was 4 years old. That gift carried him throughout his young life gaining him prestige and a chance to see the world. As the old saying goes though, that was just the beginning.

The sixties pulled George into the rock and hippie world and a relationship with Jerry Garcia and Ron "Pigpen" McKernan of The Grateful Dead which subsequently lead to an interest in heavy metal music which further lead him literally down the road to Los Angeles and stints at the Wiskey A Go Go and

The Starwood clubs. That was in the mid-1970s and Michalski's band "was headlining over such young upstarts as Van Halen as well as touring with the Electric Light Orchestra."

George formed friendships and business associations with popular actors such as Don Johnson, famous musical stars like Barbara Streisand, and was the musical director for the well-known mime comic act in Las Vegas, Sheilds and Yarnell. More than that, according to Juanis, Michalski's forte is his "uncanny ability to bring together musicians." Great musicians. Think of Bob Dylan's "Traveling Wilburys" or Willie Nelson's "Outlaws" only five times over. George Michalski has been an outstanding song writer, producer, musical director, and performer throughout his full and successful life.

You can read more about George, his work and his accomplishments on the website http://georgemichalski.com/. Oh, and invite him to the festival.

Polish or Not?

Linzie Janis, American television journalist, currently working for ABC News. She does reports on shows such as "Nightline" or "20/20." Linzie is from Schaumburg, Illinois and has a pretty and Slavic face. Polish or Not?

April 2017

Make it Better

Clean it, design it, create it, improve it, and then step back and see if you have to start over, or tweak it. Have you made something better?

Back a long time ago when I was a young czlowiek (man) totally addicted to discovering, learning, and understanding my Polish nature, I did a number of oral histories. It was a great experience and I strongly recommend it and especially for the baby-boomers whose second- generation parents and relatives are very quickly going to their eternal reward. Speaking of eternal reward, one of the questions for my interviewees was about the format for funerals. Since the Poles have great music and customs for a number of special events, I was not aware of anything culturally specific to the Poles for the funeral Mass. Is there anything?

At one of the many funerals I seem to be attending now in my old age, I realized that the popular Song of Farewell, which is taken from familiar melodies such as Old Hundredth ("Praise God, from Whom All Blessings Flow"), or O Salutaris ("O Saving Victim"), or Tallis' Canon ("All Praise to Thee, My God, This Night"), had become the standard recessional hymn of the Catholic funeral rite. The translation and words, copyright 1981, belong to Dennis C. Smolarski, S.J. It is beautiful and it moves me. The words fit perfectly with the music and are so suitable and appropriate as the congregation's symbolic final appeal on behalf of their loved one for acceptance and entry into paradise. Here are the Smolarski lyrics:

> *Come to his/her aid, O saints of God;*
> *Come meet him/her, angels of the Lord.*
>
> *(Refrain)*
> *Receive his/her soul, O holy ones;*
> *Present him/her now to God, Most High.*

May Christ who called you, take you home,
And angels lead you to Abraham.

Give him/her eternal rest, O Lord.
May light unending shine on him/her.

I know that my Redeemer lives
The last day I shall rise again.

The revision is powerful stuff and just another accomplishment for the amazing Father Smolarski. He is currently a professor of Mathematics and Computer Science at Santa Clara University in California, has a doctorate in Computer Science from the University of Illinois at Champaign/Urbana, and has written a bunch of books on mathematics, computer science, and Catholic theology.

He also has the faculties to celebrate the Eucharist in the Byzantine rite (Melkite [Lebanese], Ruthenian, Ukrainian, Russian). Father Dennis is originally a South Chicago guy and the grandson of Polish immigrants. You can read more about him on the Santa Clara University website (https://www. scu.edu/) and you can buy his books on Amazon. I am eager to buy and read his books. Cannot wait.

Mad Men Meets NASA

The Academy Awards was entertaining as always but extra exciting this year for sure. Besides *Moonlight* (and almost *La La Land*) winning for best picture, many of the critics thought *Hidden Figures* was a contender for the Oscar as well. *Hidden Figures* is about three African American women (Katherine Johnson, Mary Jackson, and Dorothy Vaughan) who helped "calculate the flight trajectories for NASA's Project Mercury and other missions." The story centers on the challenge they faced not only as women, but also as Black women in a biased and unequal United States in the early 1960s. Think of Mad Men meets NASA.

One of the positive characters in the movie is Karl Zielinski who befriends Mary Jackson. Karl is based on the real NASA aeronautics engineer Kazimierz "Kaz" Czarnecki (go figure, another Polish engineer!!). Kaz started with NASA in 1939 and remained until his retirement in 1979 as a Senior Aeronautical Research Engineer. "He published many papers together with

Mary W. Jackson serving as her long-time mentor. In 1979, Jackson organized his retirement party." My impression is Kaz Czarnecki was trying to make NASA, and the world a better place.

Wesolego Alleluja to you Pondering Poles out there and feel free to use the words to the Song of Farewell as a Lenten meditation for the presence of the Cross and Resurrection in your own lives. We will beseech God on your behalf upon your death but I wouldn't wait till then to acknowledge your short comings and resolve to make things better. To make things better; hopefully, that is why we are here.

Polish or Not?

Lori Grenier, American inventor, entrepreneur, and best known as a cast member on the reality TV show *Shark Tank*. Lori grew up on the Near North Side of Chicago and "has helped launch more than 400 products and holds 120 U.S. and foreign patents." Lori Grenier, Polish or Not?

May 2017

A Classless America? A Classless Polonia?

*I*f you are bored, you could go to a Charles Murray speech at the local university and protest him (before hearing one word) for being a racist or a sexist. Come on, it'll be fun!

Charles Murray is an American political scientist, sociologist, author, columnist, and to some a brilliant man. He doesn't make up conditions or trends; he analyzes and presents them based on his study of facts and statistics. You are free to question or debate his ideas and I am sure he would welcome that.

He is best known for his lectures and books, in particular *The Bell Curve, Intelligence and Class Structure in American Life* (written with Richard J. Herrnstein, Free Press Paperbacks, New York, New York, 1994) and most recently *Coming Apart, The State of White America, 1960-2010* (Crown Forum, New York, New York, 2012). Most of the protesting is generated by his speaking engagements for *Coming Apart*, partly because we are in an era of constant protesting but also because this book has the words "White America" in the title.

What does this book and subject, intelligence and class structure, have to do with Polonia? Murray says outright in the Prologue "The trends I describe exist independently of ethnic heritage." Sans ethnicity, those of us with European roots are part of "White" America and are connected by general European culture and society so the book pertains and includes us.

According to Murray, American culture changed drastically on November 21, 1963, the date that President Kennedy was assassinated. This date is symbolic of not how America became classless, but rather how the upper and the middle/lower classes changed and behaved and how they perceived themselves and each other. Prior to the era of the "sixties," Americans, no matter how rich or how poor, how educated or skilled they were, shared common ground in a number of value-based fronts such as community, religiosity, and finances. There was them and us back then but except for the wealth and status, them and us were singing out of the same values hymn book about most things.

Following Kennedy's assassination, the upper and middle/lower classes gradually transformed into what Murray describes as the "cognitive elite." This was when even working class families recognized "the increasing market value of brains" and the perspective of educated Americans shifted away from the traditional ways and mores of the parents and grand-parents.

For the record, the median household income for Polish Americans in 2015 dollars is $68,843 while the average median household income for white Americans is $59,698 (https://en.wikipedia.org/wiki/List_of_ethnic_groups_in_the_United_States_by_household_income). With *Coming Apart* as a backdrop, it does seem that some Americans and Polish Americans view and treat some people and things in high culture and low culture terms. We hear a lot of talk about fairness in opportunity and income. It seems to me that what Murray is positing in his book seems to be true but what will come of it?

Should Americans and Polish Americans not become more educated and strive to do better financially? Should they not be free to choose whatever cultural and values course they desire? I do believe that the "cognitive" gap that exists now will diminish in the future and my proof of this is the number of younger Polish Americans that are reawakening and rediscovering an ancestral connection. They are doing this while drinking a Starbucks, having a microbrew, or texting on their smartphone riding in their auto-piloted vehicle. Just like their other "white" American counterparts.

Polish or Not?

On Charles Murray's Bell Curve, Lana Zak has the perfect mix for material and social success in America. She is half Asian and half White. More specifically, her mother is Korean, and her father is Polish American. She is a reporter and producer for ABC News and one of her big breaks came from working with Diane Sawyer on "Good Morning America" and "ABC World News."

Among her assignments with Sawyer were the cholera crisis in Haiti, the shooting and recovery of Arizona U.S. Rep. Gabrielle Giffords, and the school shootings at Sandy Hook Elementary in Connecticut (http://qctimes.com/

entertainment/tv/bettendorf-grad-lana-zak-ready-for-new-challenge-as-abc/
article_1c22b407-fc03-5c9b-a8ff-80c33a812506.html).

One of the great hardships in being The Pondering Pole is the incredible
amount of time I spend trying to find super models with Polish ancestry. Tough
job but the hours and hours of research paid off again.

(From Ethnicelebs.com and Wikipedia) Rachel Leigh Hilbert is an American
model, best known as the official spoke model for Victoria's Secret clothing line
PINK. She has also done work for Urban Outfitters, Delia*s, Macy's, and Kohl's
and you might have seen her seen her beautiful Polish face in the pages of
Cosmopolitan, Elle, or Marie Claire.

Rachel was born in Rochester, New York, to Charles "Chuck" Hilbert and Tiffany
A. Piekunka. Tiffany is the daughter of Thomas Piekunka, the son of Harriet
Mary Bartles and Leo J. Piekunka. Both Harriet and Leo were the children of
Polish parents.

As a noted Polish culture observer once said, "scratch an East German and
you will find some Polish." I would say, give me any social or historical
phenomenon and I can find some Polish person or connection. If you like Hip-
Hop and especially if you like Bruno Mars, then go figure, you will be amazed
to see and listen to Danny Saucedo, a sensation in Sweden but becoming
more popular outside his country of birth. You can hear his music and enjoy his
dancing ability in a variety of YouTube videos.

This guy is super good looking and has a nice and appealing personality.
Danny Saucedo's mother is Bolivian (Patricia Saucedo) and his father, Piotr
Grzechowski, is of Polish descent. Danny is a singer, songwriter, and musician.
He speaks Swedish, Spanish, Polish, French, and English. If you are Polish, you
are required to speak 3-6 languages.

June 2017

"Our meeting place... "

An Italian friend told me how he gets together over the Christmas holidays with the guys from the old neighborhood. They meet at one of the most popular bars on "The Hill," play some bocce ball, and drink a little wine. The old bar is just as important as the people and it has as much character. It is just the perfect venue to reconnect, catch up, and relive shared experiences growing up Italian and as a South Saint Louisan.

The Polish American Journal makes a point to highlight buildings, churches, and gathering places in every issue. There are a couple of perfect venues in the Saint Louis metro area where people get together and "Polish is spoken." They are not in the suburbs. They are in older areas of the city, have a history, have character, and are the kind of places that I love. The first is the Polish National Alliance (PNA) clubhouse on 8201 Vulcan Street in the Lemay section of South Saint Louis and the second is the Polish Hall located in Madison, Illinois, across the river from downtown Saint Louis. Neither is very far from the Arch.

The PNA clubhouse was originally called the Stone Bar. It is made of traditional stone masonry, in a ranch or hacienda style, and the defining feature is the covered "dugout" or porch spanning the front. It is a great place to sit in the fresh air during mild days in the spring or fall. When I walk up to the front entrance and see people outside, I imagine the similar faces and looks only in a black and white photograph from sixty years ago.

Once or twice per month the PNA sponsors dinners around American or Polish holidays or special occasions. Polish food is usually prepared for the Polish events and otherwise the meal usually includes pork steaks and they are excellent. If you are not from Saint Louis you might not know what a pork steak is and those grilled at The Stone Bar are thick and the sauce is Saint Louis style. I'm drooling thinking about it. High praise to the PNA'ers for doing a great job of providing a relaxing and welcoming alternative bar and kawiarnia (café) for the Polish community and for anyone who wants to join in.

2017

At the end of April, Polish Hall in Madison, Illinois celebrated its 100 year anniversary. Historically, Madison is one of a small number of enclaves on the east side of the river that was situated between two steel mills and thus was an attractive and suitable spot for Southern and Eastern European immigrants to settle and to be close to their work. What grew from this was the standard initiative for each ethnic group to establish a "home" or a "halla" for members to spend time with countrymen and women of the same language and traditions.

Madison had a substantial Polish population and in 1912 the Alton Diocese approved the building of Our Lady of Czestochowa Catholic Church. In 1917 Polish Hall was established through the church as a social organization and in the same year joined the Polish Roman Catholic Union of America, Saint Stanislaus Lodge 1004. As the group grew, the new and current location, Annis's Tavern, was purchased in 1935. The Tavern was expanded and improved and is the structure that is there today.

This is the structure that I love to this day. The bar is made of dark wood and the lighting is semi-dark. Nothing fancy as you might expect for a blue-collar look and feel. Off of the bar is the door into the dance area and downstairs is seating for the countless dinners that were served at weddings, birthdays, anniversaries, and other events. From the history of the hall written by Henry Mulnik, "Polish Hall was indeed our meeting place for over these 100 years."

My connection to Polish Hall began when I became a folk dancer in my twenties and this is where we had our scheduled practice time. I'm not going to list all of the wonderful and interesting people that were part of our troupe Slava as I might forget someone. I will acknowledge though, my "adopted" aunts, the Turski women, Hattie, Agnes, Clara, and Helen.

It was their passion for their Polish heritage that encouraged the involvement of their kids, their family, relatives, friends, and acquaintances. I learned about Poland's Slask and Kurpiew region's dance and music and I also learned about the Polish village in Madison. One more mention and that is our accordion player was the unforgettable Wally Annis, the grandson of the man who started and owned Annis's Tavern. All of the people in this group at that place gave me so much happiness and it was my introduction to a new world, the Polish neighborhood and hall in Madison.

The 100th anniversary celebration was a testament to how much a building means to those connected to it in great or small ways. The bar and dance area were standing room only for five straight hours. There was food, drink, Dave Hylla's polka band, and a special folk dance performance by Joe Mulnik and Natalie Ruesing. What a great homecoming. I did not see one sad face in the crowd and it was a great time to reconnect with family and friends. I sure did.

Polish or Not?

Another Polish scientist!! Saw a cable presentation by Helen Czerski, British physicist, and oceanographer, and she writes and talks in a way about the kind of science stuff, like Festivus, that is for the rest of us. Her only book is called *Storm in a Teacup: The Physics of Everyday Life* (Bantam Press, 2016) and this is physics light. Get the book and check her out online. She is quite a character.

Remember Bob Ross the giant afro-hairdo'd painting instructor and host of *The Joy of Painting* show seen on public television? One of my favorite programs over the years ("Let's put some happy little trees over here… "). Recently I heard the name Annette Kowalski mentioned in connection with him. At least one website is claiming that she is the one who discovered him (http://mentalfloss.com/article/65786/meet-woman-who-discovered-bob-ross).

She was his business partner and advisor from the beginning and a painter in her own right. You can find her book *The Joy of Painting Flowers* on Amazon. Annette's husband's name is Walt, so I am sure the Kowalski belongs to him, but is Annette, who has a Polish face, Polish or Not?

Gamers w Polsce (in Polish)

I have no interest in playing video games, however, it is a very, very popular activity for some, mainly young males, mainly those still living in the basements of their parent's homes. That stat on the gamers is purely anecdotal but I am strongly guessing there also is a young lad hold up in his mamu and tatu's domu in Lublin, or Bialystok, or Wroclaw, most likely in the spare bedroom in the basement thumbing the controls on the remote with tired red eyes staring at the screen display.

There are two main ingredients for making a video game: you need a story or situation and you need adequate development. The more enticing the story, the flashier the graphics, and the more sophisticated the animation will create a more popular game. In Poland, the book series and story by Andrzej Sapkowski called *The Witcher* was the inspiration for the "action role-playing video game by the same name developed by CD Projekt RED and published by Atari." CD Projekt RED is a division of a Polish video game developer, publisher, and distributor, CD Projekt, located in Warsaw. CD was founded by Marcin Iwinski and Michal Kicinski.

The Witcher fantasy book series by Sapkowski was written in the 1990s but English translations have been published more recently. The main character revolves around Geralt, "a mutant hunter who has been trained since childhood to hunt down and destroy monsters." Who would have guessed this plot would eventually evolve into a video game! "The world in which these adventures take place is heavily influenced by Slavic mythology" and Sapkowski has garnered a number of awards including in 2012, the Medal for Merit to Culture, Gloria Artis in Poland. Besides English, *The Witcher* series has also been translated into 18 other languages. Andrzej Sapkowski is the Polish answer to J.K.Rowling (*Harry Potter*), J.R.R.Tolkien (*Lord of the Rings*), and Stan and Jan Berenstain (*Berenstain Bears*).

Iwinski and Kicinski began their foray into video gaming by translating major Western video-game releases into Polish and then progressed to creating their own work based on Sapkowski's book series and also called it *The Witcher*. The video game has all of the fantasy elements found in the novels with a "system of moral choices as part of the storyline."

CD Projekt RED released the original version of *The Witcher* in 2007 in a role-playing format. *Witcher* has been produced as a mobile-phone action game, a flash-based multiplayer fighting browser game, and *The Witcher 3*, released in 2015 "has become one of the most awarded video games of all time," and "as of March 2016, the game has shipped nearly 10 million copies worldwide." The Pondering Pole has reported how IT savvy the Poles are, and this is just another example of it.

Polish or Not?

It seems strange, especially in the case of famous people from in or around Chicago, how little we know about their ethnic background, sometimes. I happen to know based on very many years of experience, that if you are from Chicago and are Irish, that little piece of information usually rolls off the tongue and is shared right after the words, "Hi, I'm Bob… " Polish though, it seems, not so much.

Sandra Smith is another in a long line of beautiful, talented, and smart Fox News women commentators and hosts, and, I cannot find whether she is of Polish descent. Sandra Kaye is a native of Wheaton, Illinois, a western suburb of Chicago. Is Sandra, Polish or Not?

There is a link on the internet to a site called "Iconic Beauty Looks from the Year You Were Born" (http://www.livingly.com/ Iconic+Beauty+Looks+From+the+Year+You+Were+Born) and the year "you were born" starts in 1941. That year, the actress Jean Tierney is featured. Other women featured in this site included some of the most well-known and beautiful women in the Western Hemisphere such as Liz Taylor, Marilyn Monroe, Sophia Loren, and Brigette Bardot. Those are the best looks of the best looks.

Also included are a few I am not familiar with and in 1972 the woman with the iconic look is Paula Klimak. Paula, whose nickname was "Pola" was a fashion model and was very much on the cusp of breaking out into the big time. Here is a brief summary of her on a post called "Curated, The Shrimpton Couture

Blog" (https://www.shrimptoncouture.com/blogs/curated/30520833-a-model-named-pola):

There is little known about the fashion model Paula Klimak, who went by the name of Pola. She had worked in the early 1970's and was photographed by the likes of Richard Avedon, Irving Penn, and Francesco Scavullo. In 1972, clothing designer Halston chose her to be photographed alongside himself and his other favorite models (Pat Cleveland, Anjelicia Huston) for a Vogue photo spread. A year later, Fashion illustrator Antonio Lopez also picked Pola as one of his "favorite girls" for a photo posing with the likes of Patti Hansen, Jessica Lange, and Grace Jones. By 1974, Pola was about to receive her biggest exposure yet, gracing the cover of both Cosmopolitan and Vogue magazines. However, before they went to print, at the age of 19-years-old Pola committed suicide. Both magazines agreed to follow through and published the cover girl posthumously.

She is so mysterious, and her life ended so quickly I cannot find much on her pre-modelling career and especially her ethnicity. I must know, is Paula "Pola" Klimek, Polish or Not?

August 2017

All About the Cause!

*T*he general theme or lesson for this Pondering Pole is to encourage you, especially our baby-boomer friends to create that Polish bucket list before it is too late. As we push closer to retirement and beyond, legacy is what we are talking about and there are places and people that need your time and effort and places and people that you can enlighten. Keep in mind also that the list should be about the Polish things you can do for yourself and friends and for and with your family. If you leave it to chance or to someone else to do it most likely will not get done. Not being judgmental; it is just the way it is.

With that in mind, we all know the story of Joan of Arc, the Maid of Orleans, saint of the Holy Catholic Church, and inspirational leader of the French army in support of the French king, Charles VII, during the Hundred Years War against the English. She was quite the heroic woman but did you know that there is a Polish Joan of Arc?

Emilia Plater was a young woman of noble birth who joined in the Polish November 1830 uprising against imperial Russia. "Her family, of the Plater coat of arms, traced its roots to Westphalia but was thoroughly Polonized. Much of the family relocated to Livonia during the 15th century and later to Lithuania… She is described as either Polish, Polish-Lithuanian, or Lithuanian."

During the uprising she commanded a mixed infantry and cavalry unit, was promoted to captain, and though she did not fight in any of the major battles of the insurrection, she participated in a number of minor skirmishes. Emilia was totally committed to the cause and died December 23, 1831 in the manor house of the Ablamowicz family near the town of Justinavas in Lithuania.

There is a certain amount of doubt as to whether Plater's military exploits are true and some maintain that they are based more on legend than on reality. That is not necessarily out of the norm as many of our most admired figures in human history have varying degrees of mystery and legend attached to their names and exploits.

What I do like about Pani Plater is simply the idea of a young, educated, and impressive woman, in a similar vein as Joan of Arc, rallying the people, fighting, and dying for her country. Not only were Polish patriots such as Tadeusz Kosciuszko and Jozef Poniatowski models for her, but "she admired Bouboulina, a woman who became one of the icons of the Greek uprising against the Ottomans, a Polish fighter named Anna Dorota Chrzanowska, as well as Joan of Arc."

Whether she really was fierce in battle and brilliant in strategy and tactics or not, it is the passion surrounding her participation and effort in the cause that is important. Once again, Emilia Plater shines as another example of how female Poles fought for their country's right to exist and have life and liberty. And as I have said many times, it is perplexing to me why every Polish person in this country and around the world does not profess their Polish lineage and are steadfast in that reality. The love for the ancestral homeland is a mantra, on the list, to be stated each day of the rest of your life.

Polish or Not?

In the February 2016 Pondering Pole, I asked whether the billionaire property developer and philanthropist Conrad Prebys is Polish. Prebys passed away July 24, 2016 but left a legacy of accomplishment and success in making money and then giving it away to help others. He was born in South Bend Indiana, moved to San Diego in 1965, and at that point there was nowhere to go but up.

Jack Jackowski the stellar and most excellent Pondering Pole researcher, submitted the evidence shown below for the Polish Prebys.

His mother's maiden name was Maria Micinski. St. Joseph Cemetery in South Bend, (whose history is online) created a Polish burial section. Conrad's parents & relatives are buried in the Polish section, along with Stanley Coveleski, Hall of Fame pitcher. His family is listed on a website named Polish Immigrants to the Midwest.

Prebys is an aberration of Przby, Przbylo, Przybeszewski, etc., and Conrad is a fairly popular name among the Poles. For instance, my Polish born daughter in law, named my grandson Konrad.

Hard for me to disagree with any of these findings so I am safe to add him to the growing list of Polish billionaires. Now, we need the same kind of research on Terrance Pegula, the Buffalo-born billionaire.

Lucca Stanislaus, my beautiful TWO-YEAROLD grandson had a fun time at Smolak Farms (http://www.smolakfarms.com), located in North Andover, Massachusetts. Smolak "combines agriculture, education, and entertainment in a special way. The land was carved by glaciers, settled by prehistoric Indian tribes, colonized by English settlers, and now farmed by the wave of European immigrants… Today the descendants of Martin and Magdalenna Smolak and their son and daughter-in-law, Henry and Helen Smolak continue to farm one of the most progressive and beautiful farms nestled in the hills of Northeastern Massachusetts."

If you need some delicious homegrown tomatoes and vegetables, visit SF. I think I know the answer to this one, but the Smolak family, Polish or Not?

September 2017

Why Polish?

We start by waxing philosophical. Like Danny Abramowicz, a wide receiver, I'm going deep on you.

Most of the time we talk about what we do to be Polish or how much we know about what it means to be Polish. In the time that I have been writing *The Pondering Pole*, so much has changed in the world especially pertaining to social behavior largely because of technology. I think we all realize this trend will only increase. While language, culture, and history are still relevant, more and more in the first and second worlds and even in third world nations, these attributes are becoming less and less so.

The kinds and amounts of knowledge and the ability to communicate is crossing all cultures and morphing them in amazing ways. National or regional customs that were an outgrowth of human nature, quite frankly are being replaced by a homogeneous kind of consciousness and behavior that has us fast approaching a "Brave New World." The way a kid in Ghana acts and thinks will eventually not vary that much from a kid in Norway.

If you are one of the new amorphous people just described living in this country but you claim some ancestral connection to Poland, what reason would you have for any interest in Polish when there is absolutely nothing culturally conspicuous or relevant about you? Why Polish?

Here are three possibilities: 1. An academic pursuit, 2. as an act of charity to those of Polish descent or those involved with Polonia, or 3. as a hobby or leisurely pursuit. We've heard these before but let's review them.

1) Academic pursuit. If you are a teacher and need to assign a country to the class or to a member in the class, how about Poland? If you are a student at any level and need to choose to study a country, how about Poland? If you are a parent, suggest Poland as the country for the project. At one time I spent an enormous amount of time learning about the United States Civil War. I

learned a lot about it and have a certain amount of confidence speaking intelligently about it. Why not choose or suggest Poland as a focal point for your next personal subject to learn.

2) I know a lot of Poles that are worried about the fate and defend the plight of African Americans, Hispanics, gays, refugees or any number of other groups that need "help." Besides their own. I always find that puzzling because when it comes to being demeaned, or disrespected, or ignored, I can think of more than a few cases where the object of the abuse was a Polish person or Polish culture. Even if we strike the case for defense of Poland, what on earth is wrong with simply helping our own people? You know, like mentoring, or supporting, or just patronizing our Polish people and Polish businesses and Polish entities. I hate to say it, but Poles seem to be harder on Poles, sometimes, than anyone else.

3) A long time ago a young lady from Texas whose mother was a friend of a culturally involved Polish woman told me that Polish is her "hobby." Cute but at the same time I thought that was such a brilliant way to put it. If you are on the outside looking in, the spouse of a Polish person, or just bored, consider making Polish your "hobby." Like a lot of hobbies, hey, it might evolve into something even greater.

So for those all-American and ultra-modern people you know related to Kowalski that love hamburgers, hip-hop, and Irish bars, introduce and encourage a pursuit, vocation, or hobby of Polish, and then encourage it again. Then encourage it again. Sometimes all it takes is a simple suggestion. If you suggest it, or encourage it enough, they might start encouraging themselves. Why not Polish?

The Couple That Does Everything

Every city and every cultural enclave have them: they are the couple that participates in everything. Whatever it is, the festival, the dance, the gathering of any sort, they show up and they are not constrained by cliques or religious affiliation or interest groups. Their focus is on the whole and the goal is the enjoyment and appreciation of things Polish. Unfortunately, the do-everything couples are becoming fewer and fewer.

We still have several them in St. Louis, but I want to acknowledge a couple that are near and dear to me: Ron and Audrey Mueller. Ron and Aud met at a St. Stanislaus Church dance and have been married for twenty years. Ron's mom is a Wysocki from home and Audrey is Audrey Lamczyk Poniewaz, my mamusia. I wish I could give them an award for their kind of participation but there is none. Instead I would submit that we are the ones that are rewarded by their smiling faces and engaging personalities every time they show up. They reward us.

Ultimately it is the people that we love and cherish especially the do-everything couples that are in our midst and belong to our village. We love and cherish you Ron and Audrey.

Polish or Not?

Katherine "Kat" Timpf, (born October 29, 1988), a regular panelist on the Fox News Channel's *The Greg Gutfeld Show* is a television personality, reporter, and comedian. She is a tiny little thing and a Detroit girl with a German father and Polish mother. Kat Timpf, Polskie dziewczyny (Polish girl)!!

Marysia is a "luxury swimwear brand that epitomizes poolside style." The line is the brainchild of Polish-born designer, entrepreneur, former ballerina, and surfing enthusiast Maria Dobrzanska Reeves. Check her and the beautiful bathing suits out on https://marysiaswim.com. "The brand has been featured in leading publications such as Vogue and Harper's Bazaar, with a growing celebrity following. It is sold worldwide at over 100 retailers and stocked at stores such as Net-a-Porter, Lane Crawford, and Moda Operandi." Marysia Dobrzanska is doing swimmingly in her business and I am told you can find a recipe for pierogi on the website.

Another successful woman entrepreneur of Polish descent is Ula Tuszewicka, the founder and president of Tula, a maker of baby carrier products such as wraps, slings, blankets, and handbags. The website is https://babytula.com and here is the circumstance that she along with her Vietnamese-born husband Mike was presented with that eventually became Tula.

When our daughter was born, we wore her in a sling. We experienced how convenient baby wearing was and how much it benefits both parent and baby. A few years later, our son was born and we discovered the ease of ergonomic carriers. We have tried many different carriers and never found one that completely satisfied us, so we had our Ba Noi (Vietnamese for Grandma) sew us one to our specifications. It was close to perfect.

Good luck and keep going Ula and Mike. You have a beautiful family and our family is using your products and will need more soon.

"Kielbasa Hash" was on the "specials" board at the Lemon Poppy Kitchen (http://lemonpoppykitchen.net), a breakfast and lunch café in Los Angeles, California, and a favorite of my daughter Brig and her husband Alex. Katie, the proprietor of Lemon Poppy eMailed me the inspiration and recipe for this new Polish dish:

I am originally from Wisconsin, where we have a large Polish community! I've always grown up on a steady diet of Germanic and Polish food!

At Lemon Poppy kitchen we are always working to introduce foods from our childhood into the menu. My business partner is Romanian, so we also have a heavy European influence on the menu.

We source our sausages from a small sausage factory in Glendale, CA called Continental Gourmet Sausage.

I'd love to share the recipe with you! I am approximating measurements here, so if you post it, you may want to dial it in.

> *1/4 diced yellow onion*
>
> *1/4 diced red pepper*
>
> *1/4 diced green pepper (we use pasilla peppers, they have a nice smokiness to them, but you can use green bell peppers)*
>
> *1 diced potato par-cooked (we use russet potatoes, but Yukon golds are fabulous too. Un-peeled, and dipped into a pot of boil ing water until fork tender)*
>
> *1/2 cup diced kielbasa*
>
> *1 egg*
>
> *Sauerkraut for garnish (red kraut makes for pretty color)*
>
> *Salt and pepper*

In a fry pan, sauté the onions and peppers together in a bit oil (we use canola), toss in the potatoes and the kielbasa. Sauté until the potatoes and sausage have a bit of caramelization/col or. Season with salt/ pepper to taste.

In a separate pan, fry up an egg. Sunny is our go-to, but over easy is also nice!

Pile the veggies and sausage into a bowl, top with the fried egg and sauerkraut. Garnish with green onions/chives if desired.

Enjoy!

And to that I would also add a smacznego! I cannot wait to try this and I have a feeling it is going to be part of my regular breakfast "fixes." I am very eager to visit the Lemon Poppy Kitchen as well.

October 2017

Heritage for a Day, Month, or Lifetime

On August 22, 2017 the Poniewaz family welcomed into the world a granddaughter, June Aniela. She is the second grandchild for dzia dzia Edziu Poniewaz, a.k.a. The Pondering Pole, and of course she is adorable. We love you Junie Aniela and are so glad you are here!

Seen on YouTube was a 2005 interview of the famous actor Morgan Freeman on the television magazine *60 Minutes* with Mike Wallace where Freeman said "he found the concept of Black History Month to be 'ridiculous' and maintained the way to get rid of racism was to 'stop talking about it.'" Mike Wallace was puzzled that he would say such a thing and so Freeman asked Wallace, "what are you?" Mike answered, "Jewish," and then Morgan asked him, "Do you celebrate Jewish history month?" Wallace said no, he didn't as there isn't one.

So Morgan Freeman made the point about acknowledging something that from its basic sense or principle does not need recognition. If a person is secure in their own "skin," would they need specialized reinforcement that seems redundant or trite? We could say the same about the month of October which is Polish Heritage month. At this point do we need a month to realize what it means to be Polish? If you ask me, well I think you need not just a month, but a lifetime to fully understand the length and breathe of our people's history and culture and that still wouldn't be enough.

I heard a wonderful homily by a priest at the Labor Day weekend Mass. He said at some point before or after the day off, the celebrating, and the relaxing to take time to reflect on the meaning and reason for the holiday. Considering the idea of labor, how many of us actually look at our hands, contemplate the sacredness of the employment and work that we do each day, with our hands, with our minds, with our hearts in many cases, and how lucky we are to be able and willing to labor when others don't or cannot.

Heritage is like that. I think for most of us the very thought that we have a month, whether we are the only ones that notice it, is a good thing. It is a great thing really. Hopefully we will use the month though not only to relish our history and culture in temporal ways (and those ways I like a lot!!) but to go deeper in our appreciation for what we have and how far we have come in our skin.

An acquaintance had the idea for Polish Heritage month to forgo the festivities at the bar and instead read a book written by a Polish author or watch a movie with a Polish actor, theme, or story. I found that pleasantly enticing and a suitable alternative to sloshing down those Zywiec beers. As with Christmas, you do not want to forget the reason for the season, or as we like to say, like the reason for Polish Heritage month.

Polish or Not?

David Lawrence "Dave" Hlubek (born August 28, 1951, died September 3, 2017) was the lead guitarist and founding member of the rock band Molly Hatchet. Molly continued the Southern rock movement into the 80s and 90s and was known for the hit song "Flirtin' with Disaster." Dave, the Polish-looking Hlubek, Polish or Not?

Sabina Gadecki is an American actress and model and quite a looker. She is from the great Polish enclave, Chicopee, Massachusetts, and both of her parents are Polish. She has appeared in several fashion mags and on some of the more popular movies and television shows. Check her out.

We all know the sweet tenor voice of the half-Polish, half-Hungarian Peter Cetera from the rock group Chicago. Besides being the dominant sound for many of the group's hits, he wrote many of them as well. Many of the syrupy ballads that Cetera is famous for resulted from the collaboration with Steven Foster, quite a huge songwriter in his own right. Peter was inducted into the Songwriters Hall of Fame in February 2017 but was later rejected because he could not attend the inductee ceremony. Seems like a silly rule and sorry, I am still counting him a Hall-of-Famer anyway.

November 2017

Poloni... What?

*N*ations are comprised of people with like interests and a common language. Those two parts largely make up what we call the national culture. In American culture, we drink beer, speak "Angle-ish," and give our kids Irish names. America in its basic sense is a mirror of the British Isles, with roots in German Anglo-Saxon and to some extent Gaelic civilization, and those of us with lineage not of England or of ancestral English America, hold to the same traditions and political organization of those that do. Whether we speak Somali or Bosnian, celebrate Cinco de Mayo, or paint the fire plugs with the colors of the Italian flag, we feel a not-so-subtle pressure to hold to the mores of this country and pledge our first allegiance to America because this is where we live.

Throughout history, nations and peoples have intentionally or unintentionally been absorbed by others most often because they were weaker militarily or because they willingly entered into an alliance with a more powerful neighbor. These scenarios have been played out over and over in all parts of the world. American armies and settlers subdued or controlled indigenous natives and this is the example we are very familiar with.

This ties into the number of times recently I have come across the word Polonized or Polonization. The "Polonized" Westphalian German Emilia Plater is known as the Polish Joan of Arc, a "Polonized" Lithuanian Tadeusz Kosciuszko became a great figure in the war for independence in the United States and a leader for the same in Poland, and the Pole, United States former Chief of Staff, General John Shalikashvili, traces part of his lineage to the country of Georgia in the South Caucasuses. What does it mean to be Polonized or to be subject to Polonization?

To learn more there is a Wikipedia topic on it and I would encourage you to read it. The definition of Polonization in Wiki is "the acquisition or imposition of elements of Polish culture, in particular the Polish language, as experienced in some historic periods by the non-Polish populations of territories controlled or substantially under the influence of Poland." I have it burned in the history lobe of my mind that the Poles were a recognized player in world affairs but not so much the idea of holding sway over and changing other people in how they live and think. While not realizing it or assigning a name to it, I have often said that Poland did not always control Lithuania, Ruthenia, or Ukraine politically, but she influenced them greatly socially and culturally.

The reason for Polonization was the relative strength of the Polish state for the five hundred years beginning in the 12th century. During these years which included some military conquests, the Poles mainly exerted their presence by alliances with Ruthenian and Lithuanian nobility and others whose new Polishness trickled down to their constituents, servants, and countrymen. Another key factor was the role that trade played beginning with the Piast Dynasty and then with the Polish-Lithuanian Commonwealth. Many Greek, Armenian, Jewish, and German merchants and immigrants settled in Polish lands and a sizable number spoke Polish and assimilated, just as many merchants and immigrants do in our country.

Throughout history Polonization or Americanization or any other kind of "ization" has been a two-edged sword. The pressure to convert doesn't always come easily and very often it comes with bloodshed. Lots of it. That is the harsh reality. As for me, I am a Polonized, Americanized, and often times travel to and speak Southern Illinois. Going forward, my hope is that we can Polonize our relatives and friends and associates, and even our detractors, with gentle and friendly positive persuasion. Let us conquer them that way instead.

Polish or Not?

The problem with Simon Cowell is that he is too shy. Yes, that is a joke and I actually enjoy hearing Simon's opinions on the various shows. He is a television star, producer, a very smart and insightful judge, and according to ethnicelebs. com, has a Polish connection. Although he is Englishized, Simon's paternal grandmother was Esther Malinsky, a Polish Jewish immigrant.

I love watching the television game show *Jeopardy* and you must admit it is an impressive display of intellect and learning by the contestants. The thought occurred to me the last time I watched was whether a Polish person was ever one of the champions. This is a little outdated but way back in 1991 Leszek

Pawlowicz won five *Jeopardy* games. That was big because in that era there was a five-game limit on winning so there is no telling how much farther he would have gone.

Leszek went on to win the *Jeopardy Tournament of Champions* in 2014 and won numerous other game show contests bringing his career money totals well over one million dollars. He received high praise from the legendary *Jeopardy* contestant Ken Jennings and *the New York Times* referred to him as "the Michael Jordan of game shows."

December 2017

Christmas Musing and Giving, Giving and Musing

*T*o start, here is my Christmas wish list this year:

- Take a bus trip to Chicago,
- Visit the Polish Museum of America (the Paderewski Room is new, and they currently have a Kosciuszko exhibit),
- Eat at the U Gazdy ("At the Gas Station") Polish restaurant,
- Attend Mass at Holy Trinity Church,
- Shop at the KD market located in Schaumburg, Illinois in the Chicago suburbs and, back to the Polish Museum of America, see a performance by Highlander dancers and singers.

Done! That wish was already granted and realized last month, and it was a perfect Polish podroz (journey). Even if you are from Chicago and have not done any or all of these, I highly recommend you do. An itinerary for the trip can be found stated above beginning with the visit to the Polish Museum of America. You will love it.

Our beautiful Polish Christmas has a number of interesting and unique facets to it. One of them is the idea of leaving an extra plate at the table and the reasons vary, from the "unexpected guest" to celebrate the tradition of hospitality and inclusion, to "symbolically left at the table for the Baby Jesus." I've thought about it many times. The idea is a great one and whether real as for the unexpected visitor or symbolically for the Baby Jesus, it is perhaps the best way to express the adage, "the reason for the season."

The extra place setting is in the realm of expressing charity, extending a helping hand, and giving of oneself. Christmas is the time for giving. There are statistics on what demographic groups give more financially, in goods, or services. Church goers give more than non-Church goers. Red state voters are more generous in charitable giving than Blue states. Are Polish people more inclined to give selflessly than other ethnic groups?

I could not find any statistics, but the culture precludes that they do; a guest in the home is God in the home, and so on. My own policy for charity is first to help those in the family (so as not to be a burden on the larger society) and then to give outside of the family so others are not a burden on society. Others that make society better can be schools, hospitals, social aid organizations, and it also includes a wide variety of Polish entities and organizations.

One example of Polish giving is the Polish American Association (https://www.polish.org), "a human service agency" founded in 1922 to serve "the diverse needs of the Polish community." They provide a wide array of resources such as "education, employment, immigration, social, and supportive services" to the Polish community and "to others." "To others" is significant I think because it is in the true spirit of charity by giving to the "unexpected guest." Hopefully, we will hold this thought in our hearts this year when we celebrate our beautiful Polish Christmas.

Polish or Not?

What is it about a place that has produced an incredible amount of successful, creative, important, and famous people? The place I am talking about is Brooklyn, New York. Check any list of those born or who lived a significant portion of their life in Brooklyn with the creds just mentioned and you will be amazed. Any of those Polish? Hardly any but Andy Harris, born Andrew Peter Harris is worth noting. He is currently the only Republican member of Maryland's congressional delegation and his father Zoltan was born in Hungary and his mother Irene was born in Poland. By-the-way, Andy, a very impressive guy, is also a physician.

I mentioned seeing a group of Goral singers and dancers on my trip to Chicago. Besides the strolling musicians serenading the crowd, the real treat was the performance by the young mountaineer boys and girls. These kids range in age (guessing) from six or seven years old and the boys, accompanied by two of the girls, shuffled to a two foot tree stump where the boy leapt onto it, did the highlander jig, and then leapt high and with flourish off the stump. Brought a tear to my eye seeing these young kids, all born in the United States, singing and dancing their Goral hearts out. I noticed some of the boys did not have hats. They are expensive but if you want to help buy a hat or two, this website should have information about the group or regarding donations - http://www.tatrafoundation.org/.

IV

2018

January 2018

On the Greatest List.

We use the end of the year to review what was accomplished throughout the year and I think it is also a good policy to take some time to reflect on what we accomplished throughout our lives. Then we make the turn at the beginning of the New Year to map out all of the things we want to get done in the next twelve months. I remind you of this because my life is racing at break-neck speed. As the old Polish song goes, "The days, the years, the hours, swiftly are fleeting by." They are.

So, this year start with modest goals like making a "Greatest" list. Try to avoid the "Greatest Fools of All Time" or the "Greatest Mass Murderers of All Time" but generally if you focus on a worthwhile pursuit and work sixty to eighty hours a week on it, yes, you have a good chance to make it.

There are a number of "Greatest Books" lists. The Boston and New York libraries have one; Time Magazine; The New York Times; NPR; Wikipedia; and The Polish American Journal has one (http://www.polamjournal.com/ Library/Suggested_Reading/ suggested_reading.html) compiled by Florence Clowes, Book Review Editor. The one Polish name you can find with regularity on all the lists for having one or more of his novels is Joseph Conrad, born Josef Teodor Konrad Korzeniowski, December 3, 1857. *Lord Jim, Nostromo*, and *Heart of Darkness* are novels which are his most popular works appearing on all the lists. Out of all the countries with great literary traditions it is nice to have at least one Polish standout. My advice is to pick a list and read every book on it. My next advice is to read every book on the Florence Clowes list. Reading every book written by Conrad would be the kicker.

Le Monde, the French daily newspaper has published their own Greatest Books list, *100 Books of the Century* (http://www.listchallenges.com/le-mondes-100-books-of-the-century). Not surprising, there is a preponderance of French authors included on this one, Joseph Conrad's *Lord Jim* is included, but a name that caught my eye because of the Eastern European tint is Rene Goscinny who, along with illustrator Albert Uderzo, created the comic book *Asterix the Gaul*, and that is the work that made this list. Goscinny has a strong Polish connection.

Rene Goscinny was born in Paris in 1926, to a family of Jewish immigrants from Poland. His parents were Stanislaw Simka Goscinny (the surname means hospitable in Polish; Simka is his Jewish name meaning happiness), a chemical engineer from Warsaw, Poland, and Anna (Hanna) Beresniak-Goscinna from Chodorkow, a small village near Zytomierz in the Second Polish Republic (now part of Ukraine).

The premise of *Asterix the Gaul* is France in the time of Roman control except for a small village called Armorica, "whose inhabitants are made invincible by a magic potion created periodically by the Druid Getafix." The comic book is based along the same lines as famous written works from a familiar or historical time or event infused with ample amounts of fantasy and imagination. Think of *Alice in Wonderland* or *Peter Pan*. "The success of the series has led to the adaptation of several books into 13 films… "

Special for the Le Monde list, besides the token Conrad entry, there is another author with Polish roots, the great Rene Goscinny. This is also the first I have heard of the work *Asterix* but that can only be a good thing. I am sure there is a translation in English or Polish waiting to be read.

Polish or Not?

Ari Graynor is a thirty-four-year-old American actress with a highly active film, stage, and television career since 2001. Polish or Not? The name Graynor was originally "Gryzna" and her father was from Catholic family of Polish descent. He converted to Judaism as Ari's mom is Jewish from a family that also has Polish roots (http://ethnicelebs.com/ari-graynor). Her most recent film, to be released in 2018, is called *The Front Runner.*

Most Polish Americans are aware of the superb performance not only of the Polish Kosciuszko Squadron fighter pilots in the Battle of Britain in World War II, but also of Polish-American Francis "Gabby" Gabreski who recorded 28 "kills," ranking him in the top five in the United States Air Force as a fighter pilot during World War II. If you look at the entire list of fighter aces in World War II in Wikipedia you will notice at the top the name Walter Krupinski who downed an astounding 197 enemy fighter aircraft for the Germans during the war.

Krupinski was a German general in the Luftwaffe and was nicknamed "Graf Punski" ("Count Punski") or sometimes just "Der Graf" ("The Count") by Rudolf Resch, one of his early squadron leaders whose father was a professor of Slavic studies.

Resch informed him that the ending in "-ski" or "-zky" denoted a landowner, or that it indicated a Freiherr (a "free lord" in the Province of East Prussia), and thus the lowest level in the medieval noble hierarchy in the East.

Even though "The Count" was on the wrong side in the war, the 197 scores were in the top ten of all fighter pilots on this exceptionally long list. I do not know what his politics were, but I am hoping he was above all a military man who felt obligated to serve his country. One thing for sure, it is apparent he was incredibly good at it.

We welcome into the world a new grandson, Francis "Frankie" Poniewaz Schubert, born November 17, 2017!!! Frankie is a beautiful and healthy boy and mom Brigette and dad Alex are doing fine also. I can tell he is already thinking about reading all those Joseph Conrad books and Goscinny's *Asterix the Gaul.*

February 2018

Which leads to...

I watched the movie *Selena* again when it popped up on the cable network. Wonderful movie and Jennifer Lopez nailed it in her portrayal of the famous Latina star. Seeing this story compelled me to learn more about the super performer and beautiful person (inside and out apparently) Selena Quintanilla, known simply as Selena.

She was Mexican-American, but spoke only English growing up. The musical style she was famous for is called Tejano (tay-ha'-no, which is Spanish for Texas). An important thing about Tejano for us Polonians is at its core are the sounds of Central Europe. Here is a brief description from Wikipedia:

Europeans from Germany (first during Spanish time and 1830s), Poland, and what is now the Czech Republic migrated to Texas and Mexico, bringing with them their style of music and dance. They brought the waltz, polkas, and other popular forms of music and dance. However it was not until the Mexican Revolution (1910–1917) that forced many of these Europeans to flee Mexico and into South Texas, that their musical influence was to have a major impact on Tejanos.

"Tejanos" are the people and Tejano is the music that became what it is from the blend of polka and waltz tempos and beats combined with other Mexican and Spanish cultural sounds like corrido and mariachi. The accordion became an important instrument in Tejano and I have noticed how much the mariachi horns sound like the brass section of a classic Polish polka band. This is an example of cultural aspects that we think are quite different but are more linked than we imagine. If you follow the thread, Poland leads to Mexico which leads to Texas which leads to polka which leads to Tejano.

Soon after watching Selena the movie, I watched a documentary film *Murder Made Me Famous* about the murder of Selena by her fan club president Yolanda Saldivar. The documentary gave the details about Saldivar and how and why she killed her boss and idol. This led to Joe Nick Patoski who was featured throughout as an expert commentator in the film. Joe is a Texan, a huge Selena fan, and the author of a premier book about her, *Selena: Como La Flor* (Little, Brown & Company, 1996). He has written other books and articles about famous people and I would encourage you to check him out on his website http://joenickp.com. Joe is Polish, Lithuanian, and Greek, a real ethnic guy sport'n cowboy boots.

He is also very mindful of the roots of Tejano and the relation of polka in the development of this form of music. Joe and I discussed and lamented a bit about the waning interest among the young people for some of the traditional folk sounds that have come from the multi-cultural American landscape although he is optimistic and hopeful of a revival.

I cohost the Texas Accordion Kings and Queens in Houston the first Sat of every June, a production by Texas Folklife. There are always conjuntos and zydecos, and one either Czech, Polish, or German ensemble. The free event draws over 5,000 people and the cool thing is, no matter what language is being sung, or what style is being played, all the bands have accordions and all their fans dance in the same counterclockwise direction.

Alas, only Brian Marshall and my friends in Brave Combo have carried on the Texas Polish musical traditions. But there's time.

Selena said she did not care for Tejano when she first heard it. She also became huge in Spanish language music and this is for a person who did not learn that language until she was a teenager. Consider her experience especially for Polish Americans who are not taught their language in their youth and for those that reject the idea of Polish folk or American polka music. Though the future might seem bleak, "there's time," as Joe Nick Patoski would say.

Polish or Not?

Which leads to another Polish rocker? I don't know what led me to check out the rock band Rush (not my kind of music), but that generated another interesting Polish celebrity connection. Geddy Lee is one half of the brilliant (and some say genius) duo of guitarists in Rush. To hear the story of Gary Lee Weinrib, who changed his name legally to Geddy Lee, is neat for the ancestral history but also for the name. Geddy's parents were from Starachowice in Poland and survived the Holocaust after stays as teenagers in Auschwitz, Dachau, and Bergen-Belsen. His father "bribed guards to bring his mother shoes," and as you might expect, their experience had a profound effect on him.

The name "Geddy" comes from his mother's Polish rolled "r" when saying the name Gary which, as many of us know, can sound a lot like "Geddy." That is hilarious and beautiful Polish humor.

For the record, the bookend lead guitar sound to Lee's bass is Alex Lifeson who does not have a Polish connection but surprisingly an Eastern European one. Alex was born Alexander Zivojinovich also to immigrant parents but from Serbia. Another interesting twist in that he chose to change his name to "Lifeson" because his surname Zivojinovic means "son of life." Really interesting stuff for Slavophiles and lovers of things Eastern European are Lee and Lifeson.

Which leads to… one of the producers of Rush music throughout the years is a guy by the name of Nick Raskulinecz. He began his association with the band in 2007 with the production of *Snakes & Arrows*. Then, from Wikipedia:

Rush brought back Raskulinecz to co-produce their 2010 singles "Caravan" and "BU2B", and then the album Clockwork Angels, which was released in June 2012. With Rush he earned the nickname "Booujzhe", from his description of how he wanted a particular drum beat to go in a song.

Nick is from Knoxville, Tennessee but his name has a Polish look to it. Nick Raskulinecz, Polish or Not?

Poppies are red, violets are blue, Happy Valentine's Day and Love, from The Pondering Pole to all of you!!

March 2018

So Good, So Good, So Good!!!

"Słodka Karolina, dobre czasy nigdy nie wydawały sie takie dobre. Byłem skłonny, wierzyc, ze nigdy tego nie zrobia."

"Sweet Caroline, good times never seemed so good. I've been inclined, to believe they never would."

—Neil Diamond, "Sweet Caroline"

We were inclined to "believe she never would," but she did it and the good times do feel "so good!!" After 42 tries, tennis pro Caroline Wozniacki won her first Grand Slam event at the 2018 Australian Open. I cannot emphasize this enough to my fellow Polonians: trying is okay but winning is the best. And it is fun when you do.

If you were not able to watch the post-match festivities, please see the Youtube spot where the crowd serenaded her with the famous Neil Diamond song. It truly was a wonderful feel good moment. She really seems like a decent and grounded gal and is engaged to homeboy (Saint Louis) NBA All-star David Lee. With those genes I hope they have ten kids.

Pro baseball is dominated by Latino players; the NBA and NFL are dominated by African Americans; bowling is dominated by people from Milwaukee; and if you haven't noticed, women's pro tennis is now dominated by Eastern Europeans. That is cool.

The state of two (similar) unions.

I don't know if the Poles have anything resembling our State of the Union address but if they do, they could borrow President Trump's recent SOTU speech and with a few tweaks here and there, deliver pretty much the same stuff verbatim. Depending on what side of the political spectrum you are on, this is either good news or bad news and that you can decide on your own. Here is a brief summation of the status of both governments in many important areas for 2017. 2018 looks like it will be more of the same and that should in general be a good thing.

United States

1. The economy – Gross Domestic Product (GDP) hit the 3% mark for several quarters and unemployment was the lowest since President Bush II. A tax bill was passed bringing US rates for corporations and individuals very closely to Poland (21 and 35% respectively) and there were multiple regulatory reforms. The US stock market hit all-time highs and average wages for workers are beginning to rise.

2. Immigration - is an issue bubbling to a head and sometimes bubbling over with Trump's presidency and the congress. Who can work here temporarily, who is allowed to stay, and how many of each is the big question. It is a situation that has affected the United States and might affect Polonia even more.

3. International relations - this administration has challenged the idea that the United States should speak softly and carry a small stick. Instead we are speaking loudly and carrying an aggressive posture concerning trade, terrorism, and relations with non-friendly nations. There are some Americans that like the idea that the United States stands up to Kim Jong-un rather than appease the North Korean regime.

Poland

1. The economy - GDP hovered around the 4% mark through 2017 and the unemployment rate ended the year at 6.6% from 8.5% in January. Poland's tax rates are 19% for corporations and a top rate of 32% for individuals. Though "regulatory reform has stagnated," other measures such as increases in public spending, living standards, wages, and acceleration in public investment have benefitted from the robust Polish economy. On balance, the year 2017 was exciting and positive for Poland and that has made it the sixth largest economy in Europe.

2. Immigration – Poland has resisted taking refugees from the Middle East and Africa on grounds of national security despite strong pressure from other European nations. Labor shortages in the country are

a concern for the emerging economy but have been supplanted by workers from Ukraine. Who Poland allows in and for how long is also an issue for the government as it is in the United States. Despite strong criticism, Poland, along with Hungary, is holding tough on controlling its borders.

3. International Relations – while the United States positions itself as a global leader, Poland is establishing itself as a strong independent but equal player in international affairs especially within the European Union. There is Brexit in the West and Poland in the East and the EU feels a special need to be concerned with the Polish judiciary.

As you can see, the state of the U.S. and Poland stack up rather closely. Amazing and one final comparison is that President Donald Trump's professional background is business, real estate, and Prime Minister Mateusz Morawiecki was also a businessman and a banker in his previous life. Another match for these two nations.

Now for something different or "unusual."

Most of the travel brochures and tours of Poland are geared for the main sites: Warsaw Old Town, Krakow Square, Auschwitz of course, and the salt mines. I have been to Warsaw and Krakow and I want to see the other two but there are some outside the standards that are a bit "unusual." You can surf the net and find some of these spots but I would recommend you go to the web site http://unusualplaces.org. If you have been to a place which has great character, is an interesting or beautiful landmark, or has some special significance for you, let me know. Here is a few that interest me.

Zalipie, "the most beautiful village" in Poland. We hear about the legendary towns and villages throughout Europe and this one should be on the list. "A small ancient village in South-Eastern Poland, Zalipie, is definitely one of the country's top tourist attractions. Not because it has five-star hotels or massive glass buildings, but on the contrary, due to its small wooden cottages, which are painted in the most vibrant colors."

Kziaz Castle. Instead of Malbork, try this castle located near the city of Walbrych in Southeastern Poland. Kziaz has architectural beauty and history including some from World War II. "Ksiaz Castle is an impressive fortress rising up on a cliff embankment and surrounded by lush forests and immaculate gardens. With a history that dates to the 12th century, the imposing complex has had a wide variety of important owners and architectural acknowledgments that are worth a visit in their own right… Ksiaz was confiscated by the Nazis during World War II, and tens of thousands of Nazi prisoners, mainly Jews from Hungary and Poland, were forced to build a massive subterranean complex with 12-meter high ceilings beneath the Gothic and Baroque ramparts that rose above."

Bialowieza Forest and National Park. The Polish National Park is the smaller piece of the forest which extends into the country of Belarus. Like the Greek Parthenon or the Roman Coliseum, Bialowieza is a piece of antiquity that should be saved but also experienced. For comparison, eight years ago I visited Muir Woods National Monument 12 miles north of San Francisco which contains Sequoia redwood trees and under growth. I am aware of the redwoods, but it was not until I was there and walked among them that I realized how spectacular they are.

I have a feeling that will be the same with Bialowieza. More important and I do not know if this exists, but near the forest preserve there should be a vodka tasting restaurant featuring Zubrowka (Bison Grass) vodka. I believe the Zubrowka vodka distillery is located in or near Bialystok so if you can confirm this please share location and details.

Polish or Not?

Joseph Patrick Kenda is a former Colorado Springs homicide detective and the inspiration for one of my favorite television shows, *Joe Kenda, Homicide Hunter*. From Wikipedia, "Kenda grew up in the western Pennsylvania town of Herminie, Pennsylvania, about 30 miles (48 km) southeast of Pittsburgh. His uncle, father, and grandfather were coal miners; his grandfather died in a 1933 mining accident." Joe Kenda, a child from a family of coal miners from Pennsylvania, the name has got to be Polish or Eastern European but Polish or Not?

I mentioned the rock band Rush in the February Pondering Pole and one of the producers of their albums, Nick Raskulinecz. Still no word on Nick's ethnicity. Another major producer of rock and hip-hop is Dr. Luke, born Lukasz Sebastian Gottwald, September 26, 1973. He began his career as the lead guitarist for the house band on *Saturday Night Live*. He later changed his name to Dr. Luke and produced major bands and stars such as Bon Jovi, Katy Perry, Shakira, and

Pitbull. Gottwald's father, Janusz Jerzy Gottwald was an architect who was born in Lask, Poland. Billboard magazine named him as one of the top performing producers in the 2000s and according to the website Celebrity Net Worth (https://www.celebritynetworth.com/dl/dr-luke), Lukasz Gottwald is has a net worth of $100 million.

April 2018

... but words will never hurt me.

I think the world has too many laws. I would prefer people act responsibly, be engaged socially, and treat their fellow citizens according to the golden rule. We would have far fewer laws and rules if the world abided by these principles.

So now we have the new law in Poland making it a crime to "falsely accuse the Polish nation of crimes committed by Nazi Germany." Unfortunately, this new law is causing angst in parts of the World primarily in the United States and Israel.

From a Yahoo article written by Vanessa Gera of the Associated Press (https://www.yahoo.com/news/polish-law-criminalizing-holocaust-speech-takes-effect-065956365.html), here is a quick recap of the reason for the law and the opposition to it:

For years Polish officials have struggled to fight phrases like "Polish death camps" that are sometimes used abroad to refer to Auschwitz and other death camps that Nazi Germany built and operated on occupied Polish territory during World War II.

Some Poles fear that as the war grows more distant, new generations will mistakenly believe that Poles were the perpetrators of the Holocaust.

The law, however, has sparked a crisis with Israel, where Holocaust survivors and officials fear its true aim is to repress research and debate about Poles who killed Jews during World War II.

These are the two sides of the issue. The question is how, as a Pole of any religion or ethnicity or residence, who identifies with the Polish nation, and is positive about the Polish nation, responds when the charge of complicity is made to you privately or when you hear about it or see it manifested in the public square? Since the world at large has been made aware of the Holocaust this has been hanging over our head.

On almost all levels, the overwhelming evidence is that the Polish behavior and effort in World War II is very, very admirable. I therefore recommend you respond, act, and proceed in life as it concerns that part of our history in a guilt free and positive way. It is as simple as that. Feeling that way and being able to support it though is another thing. To help you organize your thoughts and fend off unpleasant charges and feelings while at the same time remaining comfortable in your own Polish skin, you can categorize the war in three ways: scope, scale, and language.

Scope

The fighting and oppression in the East were horrendous and Poland was squarely in the middle besides being actively engaged on five fronts for six years. What five fronts? Poland fought in the East, in the West, in North Africa, she fought in the key Battle for Britain, and Polish mathematicians contributed to the development of Enigma, the communication code-breaking system used in the defeat of the German U-Boat presence in the North Atlantic. You could also make the case that Poland's underground army, the largest in Europe during the war was the sixth front. The Poles fought.

Scale

If Hitler was evil personified then at least ten other European nations were allied with him, were sympathetic to him, were reluctant to confront him, or subsidized him all to the end of prolonging the war and ultimately prolonging the Holocaust. Because of Poland's willingness to stand up to Hitler, the country was virtually destroyed, the population was decimated, and the spirit of the nation was crushed due to unspeakable oppression and tyranny. No other nation in the European theatre experienced the threat of extinction and felt the sense of abandonment as the Poles. Despite the incredible pressure placed on the leaders and the populace caused by the extraordinary degree of death and destruction, Poland has the most Righteous Gentiles awards given by the State of Israel.

Language

At the core of the controversy is the popular use of the word "complicit" in describing the Polish nation. The definition of complicit is "choosing to be involved in an illegal or questionable act, especially with others." Saying that Poland the country was complicit in the Holocaust is not only not true, it is slanderous. There were collaborators and perpetrators in every European country during the war and they acted out of fear, personal gain, revenge, animus, or the worst, hatred. If someone wants to research and document the collaborators and perpetrators, go ahead but the one and only true perpetrator of the Holocaust is Germany.

In the documentary film, *The Lords of Humanity* about the life of Jan Karski, World War II spy and courier, he states at one point and I am paraphrasing, "The Polish educated and upper classes were willing to help the Jewish people but the peasantry was reluctant to get involved." There is a good reason for this: the peasantry was at the bottom of the social pickle barrel and it was evident to them that their survival was as perilous as any of the other German defined undesirables or sub-humans.

Contrast this with the years leading up to the United States Civil War. Irish Catholics living in the North, according to the well-known economist Thomas Sowell, had a lower standard of living than slaves in the South. They did much if not most of the fighting for the North in the war and during the New York City Draft Riots, they not only went after educated and upper class people who bought out of serving, but they also murdered and injured scores of blacks. Many they hung from the lamp posts and then set the bodies on fire. Irish Catholics were positioned at the bottom of the social ladder but were taking out their frustration on the people they generally were being commissioned to help. That makes no sense except to understand that people generally will lash out and blame those they perceive as being responsible for their plight. It is certainly not admirable behavior, but it is human nature.

As I stated at the start, I am not big on laws but often a law is a way to force the issue. It is probably good or necessary when patience has run out or benign coercion does not seem to be working. That is the case in the "Polish death camp" law and over time the need to defend it specifically will become secondary. More so, as always, we will be forced to defend our dignity and legacy. The law is new, but the reality is not.

Polish or Not?

Not sure if this is a good "Polish or Not?" or a bad one, but the late Douglas "Doug" Kenney, one of the co-founders of the National Lampoon magazine had a Polish mother, Estelle "Stephanie" Karch, the daughter of Anthony Karczewski and Victoria Lesniak (http://ethnicelebs.com/douglas-kenney). Besides being a graduate of Harvard and editor of the National Lampoon, Kenney was a writer for comedy blockbuster films such as *Animal House* and *Caddyshack*. National Lampoon is a national icon, but I shudder to think of how much of the humor was directed at Doug's mother's ancestors.

Joseph Kosinski directed the 2017 film *Only the Brave* that "tells the true story of the Granite Mountain Hotshots, an elite crew of firefighters who fought the Yarnell Hill Fire in June 2013, and is dedicated in their memory." Joseph's Polish father, Joel Michael Kosinski is a physician.

Viva Bianca, no, she is not Hispanic. She is an Australian actress who is the "daughter of Lee and Cezary Skubiszewski. Viva's father is a Poland-born film and television composer. Viva's brother is producer and composer Jan Skubiszewski" (http://ethnicelebs.com/viva-bianca). You might have seen her in the Starz series *Spartacus: Blood and Sand* and *Spartacus: Vengeance*. She has had a lot of work and I think we will see more of her in the future on the big and small screens.

Wishing you a blessed Wesolego Alleluja. Have a chocolate Easter egg for me.

May 2018

Boys will be boys?

"People always said, 'Why do you keep that long name? Why don't you shorten it to something?' I said, 'Hell no! That's my business! That's my name! They'll remember that!'"

—Ted Piekutowski, Piekutowski's European Style Sausage
(Riverfront Times, March 21-28, 2018 riverfronttimes.com)

*B*esides Ted, for many years Kenny Piekutowski was the face of Saint Louis' Piekutowski's and my go-to sausage guy for various personal and community events. Kenny passed away on January 4, 2018. He was a familiar and important figure in Saint Louis Polonia and really in the metro area because he was a producer and part of the brain-trust and really a guardian for the most delicious kielbasa, maybe, in the world. Do not doubt me. Kenny, good guy, will be missed.

We see and we are told over and over how tough it is for girls and women at school, work, and life in general and how they need help. There is a wage disparity, there is the glass ceiling, there is discrimination in the job, females struggle in certain academic fields like science and math, and rape is prevalent on our college campuses. This is a common belief and we are reminded about it often.

In reality the trend seems to be the opposite. On his show *Tucker Carlson Tonight*, Tucker featured a multi-part series entitled "Men in America." "Men" focuses on the many ways boys and men are lagging behind women in several categories including school, work, and societal behavior. As pointed out in the program, some of the disparities range from life achievements to tragic conditions.

The signs are everywhere. If you are middle aged man, you probably know a peer who has killed himself in recent years. At least one. If you're a parent, you may have noticed that your daughter's friends seem a little more on the ball than your son's. They get better grades. They smoke much less marijuana. The go to more prestigious colleges... And of course if you live in this country, you've just seen a horrifying series of mass shootings, far more than we've ever had. Women didn't do that. In every case, the shooter was a man.

Some of the other bad things that men "excel" at are drug addiction and drug overdose, alcoholism, suicide, incarceration, and school discipline. Women, on the other hand, graduate high school at higher rates and more go to and graduate from college. "Women now decisively outnumber men in graduate school." If the imbalance were slight this wouldn't be a concern. The truth is the good/bad pendulum is swinging wider against the guys, the poor behavior is more prevalent, and the evidence that something is wrong is there. We need to pay more attention to it.

If America should pay more attention to this situation for the boys, shouldn't we pay more attention to the progress or lack of it for Polish-American boys and men? At the least if their situation simply mirrored that of the males in the general population then we would want to be concerned but would it be a stretch to say Polish-American kids and boys in particular probably have more pressure and therefore more struggles than their non-Polish counterparts? I can think of a few ways that they do: their names, cultural bias, and even cultural attributes.

This is not a cause for panic but should at least be a wake-up call to pay closer attention to what is going on with our male children. It is also not a competition. It is not boys versus girls as we want both sexes striving for excellence. It is though, for our good and the good of society that our Polish boys and men succeed. If the template for a healthy and happy life is to do well and finish school, find a job, date and marry a like-minded and stable woman, create a family together, and develop a partnership that incorporates family and community, how are the boys and men in your family and social circle doing and why wouldn't that be the norm rather than something less?

No one can predict how life will turn out for your kids, their cousins, and friends and some would say that whatever challenges are out there makes us stronger, at least some of us. That is a fair assessment, but we don't have to expect and accept the inevitability that our boys and men are part of negative trending in the general population. The final question is not how or what will

happen to our young men, but how can we help them find meaning and purpose in their lives. We need to pay attention to the boys and men and when
applicable give them extra encouragement, guidance, and support. Perhaps
start the encouragement, guidance, and support by instilling in them a sense
of worth and confidence from their Polish ancestry.

Polish or Not?

The American Side is a 2016 movie about a Polish American "low rent"
detective who unravels a conspiracy to build a revolutionary invention. Written
and directed by Greg Stuhr, *The American Side* stars Polish actress Alicja
Bachleda. I have not seen it but welcome your criticism. *The American Side*,
good Polish film, or not? Greg Stuhr, Polish or Not?

Canadian Adrienne Pieczonka is a soprano singer who has performed on "the
leading concert stages in Europe, North America, and Asia."

*My father is 100% Polish. He was born in Poland and came to Canada as an
8-year-old boy with his parents and siblings. They settled in Saskatchewan, in
the Canadian prairies, like many Ukrainian and Polish families.*

She has won numerous awards over her 30-year career including the Paul de
Hueck and Norman Walford Career Achievement Award in 2014. Read more
about the amazing Adrienne on her website https://www.adriannepieczonka.
com/bio.html.

You see their mugs all over the mags in the grocery check-out. Prince Harry
of England and the American Meghan Markle are engaged to be married
and the person they have chosen to make their wedding cake is Claire Ptak.
Originally from California, Claire is a food writer, food and prop stylist, recipe
developer, consultant, and the owner of a small bakery called Violet located in
East London.

*I started my business as a market stall on Broadway Market, cooking from home
before opening the café in 2010. All my cakes are baked with organic flour,
sugar, milk, and eggs. Many of the other ingredients are organic as well, like our
Madagscan vanilla pods and pure cane molasses.*

Quite a woman Claire Ptak but, Polish or Not?

Jess Macallan, born Jessica Lee Liszewski, is an American actress known for her role as Josslyn Carver in the ABC drama series *Mistresses* and as Ava Sharpe for The CW network in the show *Legends of Tomorrow*. Jes' paternal grandfather was Walter Theodore Liszewski, the son of Walter Theodore Liszewski and Josephine Bronakowska. Walter and Josephine were born in Poland.

Jo Jo Siwa is a 15-year-old American dancer, singer, actress, and YouTube personality. She has appeared on *Dance Moms* with her mother Jessalyn Siwa. Jo Jo, rising star, Polish or Not?

Hope you spend just a few minutes at the beginning of May between margaritas thinking about Polish Constitution Day.

June 2018

The story behind the story.

*F*rom an article on the Yahoo ticker:

Poland was occupied by and undoubtedly suffered greatly at the hands of Nazi Germany, of course. But it does not follow that Poles played no role in the Holocaust. Far from it. As Edna Friedberg, a historian at the United States Holocaust Memorial Museum, explained in The Atlantic, "There are well-documented incidents, particularly in the small towns of eastern Poland, where locals—acutely aware of the Nazis' presence and emboldened by their anti-Semitic policies—carried out violent riots and murdered their Jewish neighbors." Worse, Polish collaborators formed a police force of some 20,000 who actively assisted German forces in hunting down Jewish people and guarding ghettos where hundreds of thousands of Jews were detained before being sent to execution chambers.

I had never heard of the police force that Ms. Friedberg refers to so I began the search for more information. In the May 2018 *Catalyst*, the monthly newsletter of the Catholic League for Religious and Civil Rights, there appeared an article by Professor Ronald Rychlak. Professor Rychlak is on the Board of Advisors for the League and is a well-known expert on the Catholic Church and the Holocaust. His books, *Righteous Gentiles: How Pius XII and the Catholic Church saved Half a Million Jews from the Nazis* (Spence Publishing, 2005) and *Hitler, the War, and the Pope* (Genesis Press, 2000) are excellent histories and a must read for every Catholic but also every Pole. I asked him if he was aware of the 20,000-man police force in Poland during the war.

He directed me to the "Blue Police" entry in Wikipedia (https://en.m.wikipedia.org/wiki/Blue_Police). This Wiki story points out a few things that might alter the impression by Ms. Friedberg such as the officers at the time of the Polish defeat were dismissed when the Germans took over, regular enlisted men were ordered to report for duty or be shot, and a number, not precisely known but possibly as high as or more than 50%, were members of the underground army or coordinating with them. Undoubtedly, some, either from fear or conviction, did what they were told by the Germans according to their code, not the Polish code. Like all great historians, Professor Rychlak leaves open the possibility that the "Blue Police" were as described at the Holocaust museum, or perhaps, not so much. Perhaps the record might need revising.

Ronald J. Rychlak is an American lawyer, jurist, author, and political commentator. He is the Associate Dean for Academic Affairs and the Mississippi Defense Lawyers Association Professor of Law at the University of Mississippi School of Law. Besides a law degree, he has a Bachelor of Arts degree cum laude in economics from Wabash College. Along with *Righteous Gentiles* and *Hitler, the War, and the Pope,* he has written several other books and articles, belongs to a number of professional and religious associations, and is in demand as a speaker. What an impressive man and resume, but wait, there is a story behind his story.

Ron is the son of Joseph Frank Rychlak, a professor and psychologist who composed a life and body of work that is powerful. Professor Joseph Rychlak is known for the study of theoretical and philosophical psychology and "he developed a theoretical stance known as 'Rigorous Humanism.' This term refers to Rychlak's argument that psychology with ecological validity should be directed toward issues that are relevant to our lives." Very heady stuff and it is obvious he was a noteworthy researcher and thinker.

Joseph Frank, born December 17, 1928 in Cudahy, Wisconsin, is the son of Joseph W. Rychlak and Helen (Bieniek) Rychlak. According to Ron, "my grandparents spoke Polish before English." After serving in the Air Force he pursued a number of degrees culminating with a Ph.D. in Clinical Psychology from Ohio State University, where he met his wife Lenora. Professor Rychlak authored 17 books and over 200 papers and served as a Fellow in the American Psychological Association as well as other esteemed professional bodies.

Joseph Rychlak passed away April 16, 2013. His entire life, career, and profession can be summed up by drive and a thirst for knowledge and like his son's, his life is an awesome story.

Polish or Not?

How about this Polish connection for Prince Harry and his American fiancé Meghan Markle for their wedding! Alexi Lubomirski has a famous name and a Polish lineage and is an outstanding and famous photographer chosen to record their engagement picture. From Town and Country magazine he also is from a princely line (https://www.townandcountrymag.com/society/g14479097/alexi-lubomirski-royal-photographer-facts):

Lubomirski was born in England to a Peruvian/English mother and a Polish/French father, and when he was an 11-year-old growing up in Botswana, he learned about his royal lineage through the Polish House of Lubomirski, which stretches back 500 years.

There are brilliant young people out there and I would absolutely consider Charlie Kirk to be one of them. Charlie is a frequent commentator on the political talk shows and is the founder and executive director of Turning Point USA (https://www.tpusa.com), "a national student movement dedicated to identifying, organizing, and empowering young people to promote the principles of free markets and limited government."

Charlie is from Wheeling, Illinois but there is not very much biographical information about him and when I requested his ethnicity from the Turning Point official site, got nothing. That usually is an indicator, so, Charlie Kirk (a.k.a. Kirkiewicz?), Polish or Not?

Another youngster in the political mix is Amy Chozick, author of *Chasing Hilary: Ten Years, Two Presidential Campaigns*, and *One Intact Glass Ceiling* (Harper-Collins, 2018), about the two presidential campaigns of Hilary Clinton. Born in San Antonio, Texas, Amy uses her Slavic-looking name rather than her husbands. Polish or Not?

Make a pledge to have a great fun-filled summer. Smell the roses, and the poppies, grill up some kielbasas, and wash them down with some ice cold Zywiec.

July 2018

"Strictly Polish – polkas, obereks, and waltzes."

What do chow mein, pizza, and polka have in common? The answer is all of the American versions are better than the precedents.

It is another one of those things that never seems to go away. Yet again I am listening to a talk show where the host makes some crack naming polka as the antithesis to everything that is cool and hip about ROCK music.

To compare polka to rock music is idiotic, but they still do it. They do it because "polka" is a code word, like "Polish," which equates all that is backward and stupid. Simply stated, American polka is the equivalent to Louisiana Creole zydeco, Jewish klezmer, or even bluegrass which are examples or outgrowths of FOLK music. Putting all of that aside, perhaps it is a good time for a quick explanation and refresher on the history and impact of this dance and music so the next time someone is railing against how pathetic is the rock group Nickleback and the only thing worse is polka, you can respond by saying, no Nickleback is pathetic and polka is FOLK music and has no relation to Nickleback. Nickleback and polka are apples and oranges FM DJ!!

Polka is a dance and it is music and it is an amazing story. It evolved to be very much a part of Polonia though polka origins are attributed to the Czech people. The name is either a derivative of a Czech word describing the beat or the steps of the dance or it literally means "Polish girl." If you use the literal "Polish girl," then most likely a Polish female was observed doing the actual one-two hop movement or some variation of it. Logic would tell me that the polka has at least some subtle link to Poland and to wider usage in Central Eastern Europe, but no one knows for sure.

In the book *Polka Happiness*, written by Charles Keil, Angeliki V. Keil, and Dick Blau (Temple University Press, Philadelphia, 1992) they found there are practically no references to polka from Polish culture. The book mentions the doctoral thesis of a researcher named Jan Kleeman, who they noted from her work, "in the sixty-six volume Kolberg collection of 25,000 melodies, she found only thirty-two that were labeled 'polka.'" The Kolberg referred to is Oskar Kolberg, the premier ethnographer and folklorist of Polish traditions.

It is so strange to hear this as my experience is very different. I asked my father what kind of music he listened and danced to when he was a young man. Big band? No, he said, "when we were teenagers and got together, we danced to polkas." In a 35mm movie of my uncle's wedding in the early sixties, the scene of the dance floor was amazing. It was crowded with guests and family, couples dressed in suits and dresses, hair styles era appropriate, many thick horn-rimmed glasses, and dancing the polka in a counterclockwise direction of course. It was so ordered and fluid and almost mesmerizing. I begged my cousin for a copy of it.

The *Polka Happiness* authors ask, as do I, "How, then, did the polka become identity music, for Polish-Americans?" At the time *Happiness* was written, "No one has yet pinpointed the moment when Polish music became truly Polish-American or when Eastern and Chicago styles are certainly themselves and not just foreshadowings of a music to come." This is not how I thought it all transpired and I am thinking most of us did not as well. In my mind, musicians got off the boat with their instruments and the people all knew exactly how to dance to the polka music they made.

What the authors of *Polka Happiness* do is outline the reasoning and progression for the phenomenon. What our immigrant ancestors did bring with them when they got off the boat were melodies and musical themes that evolved over a number of years in the early 1900s influenced by new instruments, exotic styles, and a variety of other cultures and traditions including one called American.

"The emergence of distinctive made-in-America polkas around 1928 coincided with a dual or dialectical recognition that Polish-Americans were both Polish and American, able to make music and to dance in the styles of mainstream America and yet insisting at the same time maintaining a Polish-American way of singing, dancing, and making music." This is the beauty of the story and the rest is the history giving rise to all of the great names of Eastern and Chicago style polkas. Polka is not rock, its origin is not necessarily from Poland, but the version that we are familiar with is distinctively Polish. In that sense, yes, polka is Polish.

Polish or Not?

Maybe you knew this, I did not. According to *Polka Happiness,* Arthur Godfrey, the American radio and television broadcaster, took the Baruska Polka "and put English words to it: 'She's Too Fat for Me.'" Someone needs to revise it again with a modern twist: "She's Too Nicely Full-Figured for Me."

Kazimierz Proszynski, born April 4, 1875 in Warsaw, Poland. From Wikipedia, in 1894 built one of the first movie cameras which he called "Pleograph." He was also credited with improving the film projector shutter and he devised a method of synchronizing sound and film tracks. Kazimierz Prosynski was apprehended by the Gestapo in World War II and died in the German concentration camp Mauthausen in 1945.

Also, from Wikipedia, Boleslaw Matuszewski, born August 19, 1856 in Pinczow, Poland, was a pioneer of cinematography and documentary film. Among his many accomplishments, he "wrote two of the earliest texts on cinema. They are recognized today as the first film manifestos and the first written work to consider the historical and documentary value of film." Dziekuje bardzo Boleslaw for that.

Have a happy Independence Day, enjoy the summer, and dance a polka for me. If you are a Nickleback fan, forgive me but if we are talking about rock music, they are on the "bad" list.

August 2018

"... This is the real thing."

*H*ere is more on the polka connection to Polonia.

A copy of *The Clarinet Polka*, a novel written by Keith Maillard (Thomas Dunne Books, St. Martin's Press, New York, 2002) was handed to me. Clarinet was previously featured in the Polish American Journal and now I am enjoying reading it, as a Polish American and also as an American baby boomer boy. There are many American and Polish-American references and a number of remarkable passages such as this one. It is about the first time Linda, the main character Jim's sister, sees Li'l Wally the great polka band leader and performer. "Old Bullet Head" is Jim's nickname for his father.

Just like me, Linda had grown up hearing polka music, but she'd never heard anything as wonderful as that. She said the music burned straight through to her soul. Everybody loved everybody, people were hugging each other... and Old Bullet Head leans down and whispers in her ear, "Hey Lindusia, I'll tell you a secret. This is the real thing." She said she'd never in her life been so proud of being Polish.

Like sports, politics, or any other pastime, *Clarinet* is about the people drawn into the passion and devotion of something they like very much. Maybe even love very much. How Maillard, who is not Polish, was able to capture the essence of the Polish soul is amazing.

You might want to check it out but be warned, *Clarinet* is a very adult novel, including language and content.

Got an eMail from John Ziobrowski about his research on the origins of the polka and the age-old question of whether it is Polish or Czech. Not enough room to summarize the whole paper but I will mention of few points I thought were significant.

John differentiates the specific music and dance with the genre that polka came from. From dictionary.com, genre is defined as: a class or category of artistic endeavor having a particular form, content, technique, or the like.

For the specific music and dance, he makes the point that the polka came on the world stage in the early 1800s and specifically from Czechoslovakia. There are various theories of how and why it came about. One says that a single person invented it. Another says that the Czechs were sympathetic to the Polish uprising of 1830 and in response emulated their music and dance in a large way. Here is a quote from his research paper on this.

... another music historian, Gelakovsky, in the Czech encyclopedia Masacykuv Slovnik Nauncy stated that with the 1830 uprising, the youth of Poland served as a pattern of patriotism to all Czech's. "From then on they imitated the Poles in everything," said Gelakovsky, "Polish folk costumes, Polish folk dances and songs, which were translated into the Czech language all became the rage."

So, it is possible from the Krakowiaks and other Polish folk dances the polka was morphed into what became the music and step we are familiar with. That is one spin that polka was extracted from the body of dances and music specific to the Poles.

The second and clincher for me is the logic that John used to establish that the polka truly is a Polish invention. You might recall in the Pondering Pole column from July a reference to the research of Oskar Kolberg, the consummate Polish ethnographer and folklorist, saying that in his catalog there are only a few mentions of polka. Those few mentions can support the argument of polka being Polish. Ziobrowski points out that Kolberg's *Complete Works* are all pre 1800 melodies, of which 32 are called 'polkas.' So sometime in the 1600's and 1700's the polka was developed in Poland." Polka most likely was around before the 1800s when the music and dance became a fad and there is evidence it was in Poland.

John Ziobrowski has done some stellar analysis and research on this subject and we owe him for it. Perhaps my conclusion that polka is "only" American music and dance for the Polish might not quite be the case. You might consider revising your position on this one as well. I am.

Polish or Not?

Received a letter in the mail from Norbert Dzienciol, a man who worked with and became friends with my uncle Joe Poniewaz many years ago. Uncle Joe was a one-of-a-kind character and was a true lover of all things Polish. One Easter Sunrise Mass I was the bell ringer for the Risen Christ procession around St. Stanislaus Church. As we walked up one of the long isles, I was surprised to see my uncle Joe's head poking out of the pew. As I came upon him, he gave me the "good job" nod, wink, and smile, something I will never forget.

Norbert notes in his letter the ways my uncle introduced him to many aspects of Polonia such as the Polish Falcons and Piekutowski sausage. I have stated before how encouraging friends and family to try Polish often reaps a hundred-fold in new awareness and an engaged Polonian and that results ultimately what we all live for, happiness. You can hear the joy in his letter about joining in on all the Polish fun.

Besides being a promoter of Polish things and a mentor to Mr. Dzienciol, it made me feel good to read so many nice things said about a member of my family.

Also pertaining to polka, received a nice eMail from Margaret Zotkiewicz-Dramczyk informing me of another recommended history called *A Passion for Polka, Old-Time Ethnic Music in America,* written by Vic Greene (University of California Press, November 1992). Amazon has mostly used copies available.

From the Kaminski file. This wonderful story made me smile. It is about Noah Kaminski who goes to grade school in Florida. He is the son of Ted and Lisa Kaminski and is the grandson of Tony and Alice Kaminski of Saint Louis. After the class sang Happy Birthday to his friend, he raised his hand and asked the teacher if he could sing Happy Birthday in Polish. Here is the rest of the story as told by Alice.

The teacher invited Noah to the front of the classroom and asked where he learned the song. He answered that he has a Babcia and Dziadziu who taught him, and his family always sings this at birthdays. Then as Noah began to sing "Sto Lat, Sto Lat," the teacher smiled and surprised him by joining in the song. As it turned out she is from the East Coast and from a Polish family.

Is this just the cutest thing you have ever heard!!

We are in the midst of an extremely hot summer so stay cool Polonia.

September 2018

On the list.

On this list you will find the name Darius Adamczyk (https://247wallst.com/special-report/2018/04/04/highest-paid-ceos-at-americas-100-largest-companies/2/).

We have an economy that is on the upswing and Darius Adamczyk is a Polish man on the upswing as well. In a major way. Mr. Adamczyk is Chairman and CEO of Honeywell International Inc., a company that "produces a variety of commercial and consumer products, engineering services, and aerospace systems" for individuals, businesses, and governments. Honeywell has a market cap of 115 billion dollars.

Adamczyk came to the United States when he was 11 and could not speak English. He earned degrees from Syracuse University, Michigan State University, and an MBA from Harvard University and held leadership positions with other companies before landing a position with Honeywell. After joining Honeywell, he became President of the Honeywell Performance Materials and Technologies, the Process Solutions, and the Scanning & Mobility divisions.

Darius Adamczyk is 52 years old. He will have total compensation in 2018 in the neighborhood of 15 to 20 million dollars and he will be among the highest paid execs in the country. We congratulate him on his success, wish him all the best, and want to clone him. Several corporations would like that as well.

Polish or Not?

Robert Dutkowsky is #91 on the highest paid execs list mentioned previously. He has been a "Non-Employee Director of Pitney Bowes Inc. since July 9, 2018. Mr. Dutkowsky was the Chief Executive Officer until June 6, 2018 and Executive Director at Tech Data Corporation since October 2, 2006 and its Chairman since June 7, 2017" (https://www.bloomberg.com/research/stocks/private/person.asp?personId=274992&privcapId=307265). Robert "Bob" Dutkowsky, Polish or Not?

One of the highest paid execs in Saint Louis, Missouri is Ron Kruszewski. He is the Chairman of the Board of Directors, President, and CEO for Stifel Financial Corporation and Stifel, Nicolaus & Company, Inc., a financial services holding company. Ron has a Slavic looking face and pronounces his name in the Polish way (crew-shef-ski) in commercials, "Stifel Nicolaus, We Built It." Is Ron Kruszewski Polish or Not?

Ja Ju (http://www.jajupierogi.com) is the name of a pierogi making company. "Ja Ju" is the anglicized version of dzia dziu which is "grandpa" or "gramps" in Polish. Check out the website, the story, and stalwart businesswomen, Vanessa and Casey, who make the product and run this endeavor in Western Massachusetts. I do not know what their titles are but besides being two cuties, they must be a couple of CEOs!! We wish them all the best and buy their pierogis.

An article appeared in *The First News* https://www.thefirstnews.com titled "The Royal wedding's Polish twist" by Paulina Alexandra, which claims that Claire Ptak's Polishness is from her grandmother. (Claire is the baker hired to make the cake for Prince Harry and Meghan Markle's wedding.)

The wedding cake, reported to be costing Kensington Palace around 250,000 zł (60,700 EUR) was made by American-born Claire Ptak, whose grandmother is Polish.

She has fondly noted the cooking influence her Polish Illinois grandmother has had on her career – particular the cheese kołaczki she would send the family in California.

The wedding cake is a departure from the traditional, and many credit Markle's (Princess Meghan) Californian roots as a source of inspiration. In order to reflect the spring nuptials and the Royal Family's new modern direction, the buttercream, lemon, and elderflower creation will replace the more staid fruit cake.

Her 'Violet Bakery' has become a favorite among the London set, with Nigella Lawson and Jamie Oliver both giving their ringing endorsements. Her Instagram account documents her colorful homely creations.

Ptak said she was delighted at being involved in the big day.

Go Claire!! I have a couple of follow-up questions though. Where does the name "Ptak" come from (husband) and does Claire only have one grandma of Polish descent? We wish the "CEO" of Violet Bakery, Claire Ptak great success and good luck.

As the summer winds down, my heart hurts. A belated Happy Labor Day to all readers.

October 2018

A need for culture?

*P*oles, all over the world, wake up, get dressed, go to work, and tend to family and friends. When you get down to it, all of us humans have basic needs and are concerned first and foremost with what we require to survive. This is a given.

Culture adds another dimension to normal existence. When we talk about culture, we usually mean the way we communicate, what we eat, how we dress, and how we express ourselves in song and dance for religious or temporal occasions. It gives us enjoyment, a sense of belonging, and provides a method to solidify the group that we were born into. We understand and recognize it and it is part of us.

Can culture help the individual though? Is it needed? If someone says to you, what good is it, what is your answer? Except for "it makes me feel good" or "I am following tradition" or "it is a part of who I am," what is the interior or transformative personal benefit of culture? Let me give a couple of examples of how Polish culture improved the lives of persons that were engaged in or presented with it.

The first example is about me. When I started college, like a lot of kids with heads full of mush, I went to class, partied, slept a lot, and relished the absence of parental authority to tell me what to do. That included going to church. I skipped a number of Sundays because I was too lazy or unconcerned to go. Coincidentally, I was in the midst of exploring my Polish past and it occurred to me that the Poles, who were living under an oppressive communist regime, were only allowed to go to church as a government concession rather than as a privilege as I enjoyed in the U.S.

That dichotomy finally clicked and had nothing to do with anything I learned in any class I had on my schedule. The line of reasoning went like this: Poland – communism – religion – me – United States – freedom - religion. An acknowledgement and understanding of Polish history mixed with a thoughtful reckoning of my American condition pushed me to be more responsible and go to church. Polish culture shamed me and helped me get back on track.

The second example is what I observed as a folk dancer a long, long time ago. I attended a workshop led by the great Polish instructor Ignacy "Igor" Wachowiak. For those not familiar with him, he was a big burly guy, who did a lot of yelling and stomping, and demanded a lot from his students. He wanted it done right and did not hold back "correcting" a wrong step.

There was a young lady in our group that you could tell was in search of direction and meaning in her life but knew the dance that was being taught. Knew it in the traditional way. It is important to note that she was a reluctant participant rather than there out of love for folk.

Pan Wachowiak was observing the group do the routine and then screamed STOP!! He had the young girl and her partner perform the step and turned to the rest of the group and said something to the effect, "that is how you do it!" He patted the young man on the shoulder and gave the young girl a big hug and a big smile. I could tell the praise and attention moved her in a way that made her a different person for the rest of the workshop. My understanding is she became a different person from that point on in her life as well.

There are other examples where culture provides a life-changing experience. You might remember my column on Stan-the-Man Musial where I recalled my father saying to me, "Stan Musial wouldn't act like that," and he was not talking about baseball. There is nothing wrong with wearing culture on your sleeve or having it in your heart, but you might also consider it a tool when other ways have failed or as another approach. Polish culture has plenty of heroes and material available you can use.

Polish or Not?

Brooks Koepka is a PGA golfer who most recently won his third major tournament. I have been praying for years for a Polish American to break through and win one (or more) of the top prizes in golf and Brooks is the answer to my prayers. Here is a line from an article in the Wiki Net Worth website (http://www.wikinetworth.com/athletes/brooks-koepka-wife-girlfriend-net-worth-earnings.html).

Brooks Koepka was born on 3 May 1990 in West Palm Beach, Florida. Later, his parents Bob Koepka and Denise Jakows raised him in Lake Worth. Brooks, age 28, stands at the height of 1.83 meters (6') and has weight 186 lb (84 kg).

He belongs to mixed ethnicity as his parents belong to a Polish and German origin.

This is huge!! and seems to be good documentation but I would like another confirm on the "Polish" part of Brooks. Brooks Koepka, Polish or Not?

BAKE!!! You've heard her bark that word to start bakers scurrying to beat the clock (and eggs) in the BBC show *The Great British Bake Off*. Melanie "Mel" Clare Sophie Giedroyc has co-hosted *The Great British Bake Off* as well as *Light Lunch, Mel, and Sue*, and *Let It Shine*, another BBC production.

From Wikipedia, she "was born in Epsom, Surrey, and grew up in Leatherhead. Her father, Michal, an aircraft designer and historian of Polish-Lithuanian descent from the Giedroyć family, came to Britain in 1947; he died in December 2017. Rosemary, or Rosy, her mother, is of English origin." Love British Bake Off and Mel is a riot. Check that one and the others to see her yeast rising sugar icing over-flowing personality with a cream filling of course. No soggy bottoms for Mel!

Buried deep in an article about vegetarianism, I discovered the name Scott Jurek. Scott Gordon Jurek is an American Ultra Marathoner, author, and public speaker. According to Wikipedia, he was born October 26, 1973, raised in Proctor, Minnesota, and "is of part Polish descent. He is the son of Lynn (Swapinski) and Gordon Jurek." Scott is the real deal as indicated on his website (http://www.scottjurek.com/about-scott).

Named as one of the greatest runners of all time, Scott Jurek has become a living legend. He has claimed victories in nearly all of ultrarunning's elite trail and road events including the historic 153-mile Spartathlon, the Hardrock 100, the Badwater 135-Mile Ultramarathon, and–his signature race–the Western States 100-Mile Endurance Run, which he won a record seven straight times. Scott has also taken the running world by storm with his 2015 Appalachian Trail speed record, averaging nearly 50 miles a day over 46 days–and the United States all-surface record in the 24-Hour Run with 165.7 miles: 6.5 marathons in one day.

All this and he is a vegetarian. Please read more about him on his website as there are a lot of achievements too many to mention here.

Kris Kobach, born March 26, 1966 is the Secretary of State of Kansas and is the current Republican nominee for the Kansas Governor's race. Kris's key issue as Secretary of State was to implement "some of the strictest voter identification laws in the United States," is an up-and-comer in the Republican Party, and one to add to the Pol-Am political roster. He registers a 37% Polish ancestral background with ethnicelebs.com.

Kris's paternal grandfather was Joseph J. Koback/Kobach (the son of Thomas Leo Koback and Anna Wojciechowski). Joseph was born in Wisconsin. Thomas was born in Indiana, the son of Polish parents, Jacob Martin Koback and Apolonia "Polly"/"Pauline" Czybick. Anna was born in Wisconsin, also to Polish parents, Wawrzyniec "Lawrence" Wojciechowski and Marcyanna/Marciana/Marianna Mary Landowski.

Kris's paternal grandmother was Eleanore G. Schuweiler (the daughter of Louis Peter Schuweiler and Susan/Susanne Elizbaeth Danielski/Daniels). Eleanore was born in Wisconsin. Louis was born in Wisconsin, to a Belgian father, Charles Schuweiler, and to a German mother, Margaret Sossong. Susan was born in Wisconsin, the daughter of Polish parents, Franciszek Danielski and Franciszka Peck.

November 2018

The other guy.

*T*here have been many iterations of the concept, but the original group making up The Three Tenors, Luciano Pavarotti, Placido Domingo, and Jose Carreras are the ones that I am most familiar with. Though all are well known and great artists, I must admit Pavarotti and Domingo are the two that I recognized, and Carreras was unfortunately "the other guy." You might also recall the Seinfeld episode about The Three Tenors and the same Carreras being "the other guy." It was hilarious.

The remains of Prince Jozef Antoni Poniatowski "were transported to Poland in 1817 and buried in the cathedral on Krakow's Wawel Hill, where he lies beneath Tadeusz Kosciuszko and John III Sobieski." I am guessing, but even if you are fairly well versed on Polish history, Prince Jozef compared to the other two might make him fall into the category of, well, "the other guy." Being that guy is not a bad thing and, in this case, actually makes for a nice opportunity to acquaint or reacquaint you with a real patriot and leader like Poniatowski. November 11, 2018 is the 100th anniversary of the rebirth of The Second Polish Republic and therefore there is no better time to do it.

He was born May 7, 1763 and was "a nephew of King Stanisław II Augustus and his military career began in 1780 in the Austrian army, where he attained the rank of a colonel. In 1789, after leaving the Austrian service, he joined the Polish army. Poniatowski, in the rank of major general and commander of the Royal Guards, took part in the Polish–Russian War of 1792, leading the crown forces in Ukraine, where he fought a victorious battle of Zielence."

He fought along Kosciuszko in the Kosciuszko Uprising of 1794, fought and won battles for the Duchy of Warsaw, and won a number of battles in the Austro-Polish War that "ended with a Polish victory which allowed the Duchy to partially recover lands once lost in the partitions of Poland."

With the rise of Napoleon Bonaparte and the Polish alliance with the French during his reign, Poniatowski and his army became part of the French invasion of Russia. During the battle for Moscow, Prince Jozef was wounded and returned to Warsaw to recuperate. His final major campaign on behalf of Napoleon and ultimately for the benefit of Poland was in the Battle of Leipzig, also known as the Battle of the Nations. One of the bloodiest battles in history, Jozef Poniatowski was wounded and drowned in the Elster river.

There are many attributes about this man that we can admire and emulate. He was dedicated to regaining the life and respect of his country by fighting for it. He didn't just "try" hard, he was a fierce warrior and won many battles often when he was greatly out resourced and outnumbered. He was a true leader even to the point of often being at the head of the charge. If you know a young Polish boy or girl that needs an example of heroism, the name Prince Jozef Antoni Poniatowski is a worthy choice and perhaps one not as well known.

Polish or Not?

In the March 2018 Pondering Pole, I asked whether Joseph Patrick Kenda, the former Colorado Springs, Colorado homicide detective and the inspiration for the television show, *Joe Kenda, Homicide Hunter* is Polish, or not? "Kenda grew up in the western Pennsylvania town of Herminie, Pennsylvania, about 30 miles (48 km) southeast of Pittsburgh. His uncle, father, and grandfather were coal miners; his grandfather died in a 1933 mining accident."

Per Denise Hoover of the Colorado Springs Police Department, Joe in an eMail "responded that he is Slovenian on his father's side and there is no Polish connection." We can thus conclude, Joe Kenda is a homicide hunter and an Eastern European but not a Pole. Though I will maintain he still looks like Polish Chester K. from Saint Louis.

What we have seen in the last two or three decades is the rise of cooking shows of all kinds. Beat Bobby Flay "is an American cooking competition on the Food Network" starring Bobby Flay, an "Iron Chef," restaurateur, and reality television personality. Various well-known, popular, and "buddie" chefs compete against Bobby Flay and if you look at the list of those who have challenged him, many of the names are Polish. I happened to watch one of the episodes from February 2018 where Chef Mike Andrzejewski of Buffalo, New York beat the Flay!

In an interview appearing in the *Buffalo Eats* food magazine (http://www. buffaloeats.org/2011/12/12/buffalo-foodies-mike-andrzejewski/) it was apparent that Mike is a credible chef and restauranteur. One question asked was about Mike's dining preferences. I know he is a Polish guy because one of his favorite restaurants was a place called Bistro Europa:

For dinner I got the Kielbasa with lazy pierogi ($12)… The kielbasa was amazing, it was literally dripping (it was that juicy) when it was served. The lazy pierogi (which I didn't know what it was until I ate it) was alright but nothing amazing. I would have preferred real pierogis. They also had some spicy mustard that might have been homemade, either way, it was fantastic. It definitely had a bite to it but was perfect with the sausage.

Props to Mike Andrzejewski for his great work as a chef and outstanding performance on *Beat Bobby Flay!!*

The Second Polish Republic was created November 11th, 1918. If you have even one sliver of Polish in you, I am hoping you take just a moment and think how incredible this historical event was for the millions like you and for the benefit of the world. It is good that people with a common history, language, and culture have the right to self-determination. Pray for and support the Polish people and the Polish nation. Long live Poland! Boze Zbaw Polske!!

December 2018

Sometimes dreams do come true.

"The current political and social situation in Poland and this Prime Minister are what I had hoped it would be."

— Solidarity Member

*T*hose are not the words verbatim, but it is certainly representative of sentiments for what Poland is today compared to what it was when the Solidarity movement opposed the Communist authorities and Soviet domination of the country in the 1980s. The words are thought provoking.

A wide variety of the Saint Louis Polonia celebrated Polish Independence Day at the Polonez Ball held at the Chase Park Plaza Hotel, November 3rd, 2018. By my estimate there were at least ten Polish organizations or representatives present at this event. I am not going to list any of them for fear of leaving someone out.

The Ball is always a special event every year but this year it was more special. The connection between the 100th anniversary and the remarkable transformation of the Polish nation are noteworthy. After 100 years, Poland is now a secure and stable place for the people living there and for those of us in the diaspora it is now a comfortable place to go home to. The economy, the government, and the living conditions for the Polish people are good and getting better.

For example, the GDP (Gross Domestic Product; the amount of good and services produced in an economy) for Poland is around 600 billion, good enough according to *Statistics Times* (http://statisticstimes.com/economy/countries-by-projected-gdp.php), to rank as the 22nd largest economy in the world. This is just one indicator though an important one that is strong for citizens, good for those interacting and doing business with the Poles, and conducive for attracting visitors and tourists.

It is the end of the year; Thanksgiving is just behind us and soon we will celebrate Christmas Wigilia. It is a good time for reflection and whether you are a Pole from Poland who lived through wars and oppression or a Pole from the United States vicariously experiencing an ancestral homeland far away, it is a breath of fresh air for that place to be a free and independent part of the world community. It isn't a dream anymore and we have so much to be thankful for.

Polish or Not?

Matt Mackowiak is the president of the Potomac Strategy Group (https://www.potomacstrategygroup.com) with offices in Austin, Texas, and Washington, D.C. Potomac "provides political consulting to conservative campaigns and media relations and crisis communications assistance to companies, groups and individuals." He has appeared on numerous talk shows for his expert analysis and does speaking engagements analyzing and previewing state and national elections.

Matt has been successful though as a consultant in several elections in the State of Texas. Here is a recent example:

In the 2018 cycle, Matt served as General Consultant for Pete Flores, who won Texas Senate District 19 in a 'shocking' and 'historic' 53%-47% win over Pete Gallego in the September 18 special election. Flores flipped a D+12 district and became the first Hispanic Republican ever elected to the Texas Senate. In just eight weeks, the Flores campaign and their supporters made more than 100,000 calls, knocked on more than 30,000 doors, raised over $350,000 and the candidate visited all 17 counties. Flores' current term will end in January 2019.

There are other successes so please visit the Potomac Strategy Group website to learn more about what the group and Matt Mackowiak are doing. You can also YouTube Matt to experience how he presents himself on television and radio. He presents very well, and it is evident that he knows about what he speaks. We wish him all the best.

My brother Greg and sister-in-law Jane visited Prague and Krakow this past October. This was their first venture to Poland, and I could not wait to hear their impressions of the "new" Poland. It is always good to get feedback on anything and here are a few sentences about their trip. You might notice how well it mirrors the theme leading off this Pondering Pole column.

When we flew from Prague to Krakow, we weren't sure what to expect---probably more of a dour, Eastern European or Russian sort of culture and experience. We were pleasantly surprised.

From the moment our cheerful driver, who spoke no English, greeted us at the airport and drove us to our little hotel in Old Town, we experienced only smiling, welcoming, helpful people.

The lovely ladies working reception at the Wit Stwosz Hotel were always friendly and jumped to make arrangements for us. Even the waiters we encountered at restaurants showed good humor and a desire to please.

Having just flown from Prague, a beautiful old city, we immediately noticed how incredibly clean Krakow was. During our time in Old Town and touring historical sites, I never saw one piece of trash! Prague was a wonderful city, but graffiti covered buildings everywhere. Not in Krakow! The Poles we met were immensely proud of their lovely old city. We noticed a remarkable respect for Krakow and pride of its history from everyone we talked to.

They were delighted with so many other parts of the trip too numerous to list here but it included comments about the square, the buildings, the food, and seeing the salt mines. I had a boss once who said, "I don't want to visit any place where they don't want me to be there." Based on what Greg and Jane experienced I think the Polish people want you there. I cannot wait to go myself again!!

2019

January 2019

That's What I'm Talking About!

*T*he purpose of The Pondering Pole is not only to inform about impressive, notable, and successful people, places, and events with a Polish connection, but more importantly, it is to influence and demonstrate to individuals that they also, hopefully, can be as impressive, notable, and successful as well. If you are still living in mom and dad's basement and spending most of your time playing video games and staring at a poster of Casimir Pulaski (or perhaps Emily Ratajkowski) then you don't get it. Wherever you are or whatever your station or circumstance, you can do it Polonia! You can make a difference and be successful. Here are three great examples to consider and emulate.

Maybe you saw the ad running up to the Thanksgiving holiday sponsored by the Polish National Foundation (http://www.wgtatv.com/clip/14682543/polish-national-foundation-announces-veterans-day-ad-buy-in-united-states) showing four modern-day Polish soldiers who fought alongside American troops in Iraq, Afghanistan, and other theatres, speaking about the 100th anniversary of Poland's independence.

The three men and one woman of the Polish military "salute" and thank America for being directly responsible for the 2nd Polish Republic created after World War I (from the Woodrow Wilson 14-Points principles for peace). Just as important though, this is a great example on how to affect American opinion and hit a nerve. Please watch this video as it will tug at your heart strings. It moved me and I can't imagine that others did not notice and were not moved as well. Thanks to the Polish National Foundation for thanking us.

Back in 2012 The Pondering Pole featured a company called Terra Chips (http://www.terrachips.com). The founders of that company were Dana Sinkler and Alex Dzieduszycki, two former Manhattan four-star restaurant chefs that left their jobs to start a catering company which eventually became Terra Chips. Terra Chips was bought out by TSG Consumer Partners and Alex subsequently moved on to start Alexia Foods that was a company "positioned as a healthy alternative to the Ore-Ida potato products in the freezer case."

Coming off the success of Alexia and apparently aware of the old adage, "third time is a charm," Dzieduszycki embarked on a new adventure starting a specialty pastry and bread company named after his son called Julian's Recipes (https://www.juliansrecipe.com). Our house currently has a big bag of Terra Chips in the pantry as my wife Sue loves them. There is information on the web about the various aspects of Alex Dzieduszycki's success as an entrepreneur. I would encourage you to read about this amazing guy and how he got to where he is today.

So Alex Dzieduszycki is an entrepreneur and Alina Morse is, wait for it… new word, kidpreneur! Here is a brief summary of her story:

When Alina Morse was seven years old, she went to the bank with her dad and the teller offered her a lollipop. While she really wanted to accept, her parents always told her that candy was terrible for her teeth. So she asked her dad, "Why can't we make a lollipop that's actually good for your teeth?" And in that moment the idea for Zolli-pops® was born!

This is another great story about dad-daughter collaborations. It was her father that helped Alina create "lollipop treats that were actually good for teeth." Why Zollipops? The name for the treats, "Zollipops" also came from a family member. As her little sister attempted to pronounce lollipop, it came out sounding like zollipop and that struck a chord with Alina. The name was unique and she wanted something unique.

Zollipops has a website and read how this Polish-American youngster has made a difference (https://zollipops.com). At the same time, you can place your order for a thousand Zollipops.

Polish or Not?

Lucianne Walkowicz (under the category of "gorgeous lady scientists") is a commentator in the new National Geographic series *Mars*. She is an "an American astronomer based at the Adler Planetarium noted for her research contributions in stellar magnetic activity and its impact on planetary suitability for extraterrestrial life." That is a mouthful and she has quite an impressive resume. Lucianne "Copernicus" Walkowicz, Polish or Not?

So, you think Gronk (Rob Gronkowski, tight end for the New England Patriots) can carry a team and is the best? What about Travis Kelce of the Kansas City Chiefs? Travis is a rather good tight end as well, the name Kelce looks similar to Kielce, a city in Southern Poland, and he was born in Cleveland Heights, a suburb of Cleveland, Ohio. His ethnicity seems to be a mystery on the net. Travis, Polish or Not?

Jak szybko mijaja chwile and Happy New Year!! I hope 2018 was a good one for you. Whatever the case, good luck this year; I hope it is healthy, happy, and productive. Remember Polonia, success is just around the corner. Figure out a way to produce your own poignant commercial, specialty Food Company, or a healthier substitute for sugary candy. Make 2019 the year that you do it.

February 2019

A Medley of Inspiration

*I*f you think the accomplishment of Alina Morse, creator of Zollipops and featured last month in the Pondering Pole was amazing, well, let me tell you about the rest of her family! Alina truly is a brilliant young Polish American kidprenuer but as her father Tom pointed out in our subsequent eMail correspondence, she comes from a line of some highly creative and enterprising people. Here is a sample:

Alina's grandfather Henry Starr (his father was originally named Starzynski) was 100% Polish and also started and ran his own advertising agency in Detroit for approximately 20 years. He also invented several games, and most notably was the promoter of the first truck bed liners, which is still the leading brand in the space today.

Alina's great grandfather, Alex Root (Pop-Pop, originally named Alex Rysukewicz), from Pinsk, Poland, came through Ellis Island with a pierogi board on his back. He was an inventor, a cartoonist, a wrestler, and was a World War I pilot. In 1920, at 20 years of age, Alex opened the first Root's Garage. Then later in his early 30's he opened Mt. Elliot Tool and Machine Company that was in business 48 years. It made certain parts for automobiles – one of which was the "Root Shake-Proof Lock."

Alina's great uncle, George Root, opened Ramco Products, also automotive related, and was in business 30 years.

Her great aunt, Victoria Kowalska, opened Henry's Lounge Bar/ Restaurant and owned that business for 30 years.

Okay, three comments about this particular family tree. 1) Again, Alina is the product of some really great genes, 2) the people in her family understood and took advantage of American opportunity and the free market system to take risks, succeed personally, and contribute to the betterment of the country, and 3) we are glad Alina and the Morse family are continuing with the same energy and enthusiasm for the American way and the way of her Polish ancestors that made America their home. Not everyone can come from the same kind of outstanding family, but you can start your own. Put a pierogi board on your back and make it happen!

Stas'

The Netflix station is featuring the Leonardo DiCaprio produced documentary *Struggle: The Life and Lost Art of Szukalski* about the life of the Polish born artist, Stanislaw Szukalski. There is a lot of information packed into this program and suffice to say Stanislaw Szukalski was a talented and complicated guy. Some say he was a genius, some say a bigot, and some say both. After watching the show, I'm not sure how to judge his heart but I urge you to watch this documentary at the least because he was a fascinating person, and this is a fascinating story.

Struggle, directed by Irek Dombrowolski is really about the rediscovery of Szukalski by artist Glen Bray and his wife Lena Zwalwe who were made aware of his (largely unknown in America) work in the early 1970s. The Brays along with George DiCaprio, the father of actor Leonardo DiCaprio were amazed at the greatness and power of the work and took steps to propagate his artistic legacy to the California and American public and fine arts community. Their interaction and interviews record the purpose and methods he used primarily as a sculptor, record his theories on Zermatism (the source and kinds of human expansion across the globe), and touch on his political activism leading up to World War II.

Any honest researcher will report the achievements and the faults of some of the greatest figures in world history. Glen Bray and the other friends and acquaintances of "Stas'" Szukalski did not shy away from talking about his troubling actions and weird ideas. They were not sure how to take Zermatism, rolled eyes at his outlandish and mean statements about other artists and nationalities, and to the charge of anti-Semitism, it was George DiCaprio that said Stanislaw Szukalski "shape-shifted to suit the situation."

That last sentiment is most likely the true mindset, but it is still terribly disappointing especially for a guy who was a good friend of the famous Jewish Hollywood personality Ben Hecht in his early days in America. According to Glen Bray, "In over 200 hours of taped interview, I did not hear one anti-Semitic word come out of Stas's mouth." Stas' was multifaceted in art and in life. See the movie.

Polish or Not?

Oh, Miss Canada!! Placing in the top ten in the 2018 Miss Universe Pageant was Miss Canada contestant Marta Magdalena Stepien. Besides winning Miss International Canada 2017, the Polish-born Canadian model was crowned Miss Universe Canada 2018. "She is a student of Biomedical Engineering Technology at St. Clair College and is an applied researcher. She speaks French, Polish, German and English." Beauty and brains.

Marta garnered high praise from a commentator in the swimsuit competition who said, "she has a great, easy, relaxed kind of glamor about her." After some extremely focused, easy, and relaxed research of her glamor and the glamor of the whole 2018 swimsuit field (and suffice to say it was an arduous assignment), I definitely would agree with that assessment.

The name Victor Skrebneski popped up on the Yahoo ticker last year for a reason I have since forgotten but pegged him as a big deal and in a 2016 article he was "called Chicago's best-known advertising photographer." He "shot famous campaigns for Estee Lauder, Chanel, and Givenchy, among others. He's also known for his black-and-white portraits of celebrities including Dennis Hopper, Betty Davis, and Sharon Stone."

In this same article (http://www.chicagotribune.com/entertainment/chicagoinc/ct-cindy-crawford-victor-skrebneski-20160913-story.html) a small time and not very well known model called Cindy Crawford (!) "credits Skrebneski with teaching her how to hold her body, show off the clothes, work with the camera, and pay attention to the light." Victor told her she "didn't have an easy face to photograph" but she praised him as the "only photographer that knew how to make her look good." Hmmm. Cindy, define "look good."

Per Wikipedia, Victor Skrebneski was born to parents of Polish and Russian heritage.

Happy Valentine's Day and be sure to do something nice for your sweetheart. Do something nice for someone anyway.

March 2019

Where is the Polish Architectural Capital?

*F*or this question on *Jeopardy!* the answer would be: What is Gliwice?

In an article published in December of 2014 entitled *A Foreigner's Guide to Polish Architecture* (https://culture.pl/en/article/a-foreigners-guide-to-polish-architecture), the author Anna Cymer explores several perspectives on the history, state, and styles of architecture present in Poland. There are eight chapters in this rather long piece but the one that I was especially interested and with the most to offer is the region of Silesia, especially the city of Gliwice. As Anna Cymer says:

Tracing the development of Polish architecture in the 20ᵗʰ and 21ˢᵗ centuries, one can easily notice that it is neither the Warsaw nor the Krakow area that boasts the most interesting endeavors, but the southwestern region of Silesia. This is where the architectural heart of Poland beats the quickest. It is the home of some of the best Polish talents in the field, and a region where numerous projects by renowned architects were also realized.

The Architecture Department of the Silesian Polytechnic was founded in 1945, with its headquarters in the city of Gliwice. For years, the school in Gliwice has been known to educate the most talented among Polish architects, always employing the most modern and innovative trends in its program.

There are a number of possible reasons that this part of Poland emerged as a hub for quantity and creativity in building after World War II. Since Silesia was shared German/Polish ethnically before the war, the amount of destruction was less intense than in other more predominantly Polish sectors and therefore many historical structures were spared in cities such as Gliwice, Bytom, and Zabrze.

And because of the incredible decimation of the Polish economy during the war and since mining was still an intact and viable industry in this region, the communist authorities used this area to showcase the new modern socialist community. With that new "worker" came new living quarters and other structures to go along with the new ideology or counter-ideology in the case of the number of Catholic churches constructed in defiance to that movement.

The Spodek stadium in Katowice is an example to accommodate the secular masses and the Church of the Holy Spirit in Tychy, Church of Christ the Redeemer in Czechowice Dziedzice, and the Church of Divine Charity in Krakow represented conspicuous shrines opposing communist dominance. Cymer mentions several outstanding architects such as Tomasz Konior, Robert Konieczny, Stanislaw Kwasniewicz, and Stanislaw Niemczyk leading the way in these and other projects.

American television stations are loaded with shows about all kinds of home and building design and I love watching them. This topic presents another twist on that theme. You will learn something reading this article.

Polish or Not?

Now available on Netflix, *Springsteen on Broadway*. Over the years there have been hints that the Pondering Pole is a big-time Springsteen fan. Actually, I have been one since *Born to Run* debuted while I was in college. In *On Broadway*, Bruce talks about his life on the Jersey Shore and the people and places that formed him personally and professionally. Two of those people influencing his rock n' roll awakening were Walter and Raymond Cichon (pronounced "she-shown" by Bruce).

And it made me think about my own friends from back home. Walter Cichon. Walter Cichon was the greatest rock n' roll front man on the Jersey Shore in the bar band '60s. He was in a group called the Motifs, and he was the first real rock star that I ever laid my eyes on. He just had it in his bones. He had it in his blood. It was in the way that he carried himself. On stage, he just was deadly. He was raw and sexual and dangerous, and in our little area he taught us, by the way that he lived, that you could live your life the way you chose.

Walter had a guitar-playing brother, Raymond. Raymond was tall, tall, kind of a sweetly clumsy guy; one of those big guys who just aren't comfortable with his size... Raymond was my guitar hero. He was just a shoe salesman in the day. And, uh, Walter, I think, worked construction. They were only a little bit older than we were, never had any national hit records, never did any big tours, but they were gods to me. And the hours I spent standing in front of their band, studying, studying, studying, class in session. Night after night, watching Ray's fingers fly over the fretboard, and Walter would scare the **** out of half the crowd. Oh man, they were essential to my development as a young musician. I learned so much from Walter and from Ray. And my dream, my dream was I just wanted to play like Ray and walk like Walter.

So, there are several references on the web that the name Cichon is Polish, but can anyone confirm Walter and Ray Cichon, Polish or Not? Also, perhaps a Polish American Journal reader who hung out on the Jersey Shore and was familiar with The Motifs during the 60s can substantiate the claims made by Springsteen. I would like to hear if it were true what "The Boss" is saying about Walter and Ray.

Think about it. If the Cichon brothers were all or part Polish, perhaps the greatest rock song writer and performer in American history dreamt to "play like Ray and walk like Walter."

I generally don't like to drill down this much, but last year two Massachusetts State Senators of Polish descent, Stephen Kulik, D-Worthington, and John Scibak, D-South Hadley, retired after a combined 41 years of public service. In an article in the Daily Hampshire Gazette dated 12/14/2018, the author Patrick Lovett quotes Matt Szafranski, editor-in-chief for Western Massachusetts Politics & Insight as saying "The impressions they left have been unambiguously positive... They were dedicated to the issues people in their districts cared very deeply about... areas that are very much activist communities felt like they had a voice." In our charged political times, may these two individuals be models for future representatives and, for representatives of Polish ancestry.

Depending where you live, Spring is here or just around the corner so send in your seed order for the "Polish Tomato." Check out the book *Epic Tomatoes: How to Select and Grow the Best Varieties of All Time*, where the author Craig Lehoullier "states that 'Polish'... will always hold a special place in my tomato-themed heart... "

April 2019

Go West, Young Pan!

A list can easily be made for many of the "halls," "homes," cultural centers, or even popular watering holes in the major Polish urban centers in the United States. Typically, foreign nationals with different languages and traditions will congregate together and it is usually in a physical place. Some are very old and others newer depending on the immigrant era and specific group. It is also the kind of thing that is always evolving.

I had a discussion with a friend recently about the absence of such a place in the Los Angeles, California area and I do not believe there is one in San Francisco either. That is a shame, perhaps, but to my surprise in researching what is out past the plains are a number of Polonian halls, homes, or cultural centers in other major cities beginning with Denver and extending to the West Coast. Below is a list of some of them; the information is taken from the individual websites but at least this might be a starting point if you are visiting or touring these cities and need a cultural fix or if you are just curious about what the other side of the continent is doing, or did. I have listed the name, address, website, and a brief description or history of the organization or facility.

Pulaski Club of Arizona, Phoenix, Arizona

4331 East McDowell Road, Phoenix, AZ 85008

https://www.pulaskiclubaz.org

The Pulaski Club was organized in May 1939. From the website:

Pulaski Club is the only Polish/American social club in the Central Phoenix area and the only club in the entire Valley of the Sun with our own Club House, bar and kitchen. We're looking forward to another year of great dancing and great dining!

Polish Club of Denver, Denver, Colorado

P3121 West Alameda Avenue, Denver, CO 80219 (303-934-3955)

http://www.polishclubofdenver.com

The website is in the Polish language so if you can read what is going on this might be the right place for you. If you cannot, this still might be the place for you. See the "News" section for activities they are promoting and advertising.

Polish Hall Portland, Oregon

3832 N. Interstate Avenue, Portland, OR 97227 (503-287-4077)

http://portlandpolonia.org

Polish Hall in Portland was built in 1914 and is on the Portland Historical buildings register. That alone might be worth the effort to see and experience.

Polish Home of Seattle Seattle, Washington

1714 18th Avenue, Seattle, WA 98122 (206) 322-3020

https://www.polishhome.org

The Polish Home Association has celebrated 98 years of establishment. The Hall is a place for celebration, festivals, meals, meetings, and evolving into new generations. Today, as yesterday, it is a hub of activity and a place for people of Polish nationality and descent to come together and celebrate common ground.

On a side note, we are blessed in Saint Louis to have a few venues that have the Polish stamp on them. I have mentioned the 100th anniversary of Polish Hall located in Madison, Illinois and the Polish National Alliance clubhouse located in the Lemay neighborhood in south city in past Pondering Poles. There is also the Polish Heritage Center (PHC) located at Saint Stanislaus Church in North Saint Louis. The PHC is modern banquet facility that not only serves the congregation for town hall meetings, festivals, birthdays, weddings, and other special events but it is a popular spot for non-members and especially for those living in the current neighborhood around the church.

This is now but I also want to reminisce and mention that there actually was a Polish Hall located down the street from Saint Stanislaus (at the corner of Cass Avenue and 20th Street) that was the gathering place for the original Polish enclave surrounding the church at the turn of the twentieth century. It no longer exists but like all "halls" or "homes," there was music, dancing, drinking, and food, and Polish was spoken.

"It was such a functional place," said Mary Ann Szydlowski, former president of the Polish American Cultural Society who debuted her singing career there. "As you walked in the entrance the exceedingly long bar extended down the left wall. The main area featured a high ceiling over an area that could accommodate well over 300 guests. There was a main stage along with adjoining areas for small productions or meetings. The kitchen was in the basement and the building even had living quarters for staff members."

All the folks from my parent's era (Edward Poniewaz and Audrey Lamczyk met at Polish Hall) often mentioned it. They loved that place and miss it. That was where the action was, where friends and lovers could socialize and dance the night away. I can see it in my mind's eye and imagine it like it was yesterday.

Polish or Not?

Names. Perhaps you also heard this mentioned during the NCAA National Football Championship game that one of the coaches on the Clemson Tigers is a man named Lemanski Hall. Mr. Hall appears to be an African American but his first or given name is a Polish surname. Fascinating and is there a Polish, or not, or what, connection? Why Lemanski, Lemanski?

Another name that looks Polish but points to a non-Polish person is "Kiesza." There is a Canadian pop singer called "Kiesza" but her real name is Kiesa Rae Ellestad. She is more Scandinavian than anything else. "She added the 'z' because she "was just a weird child – my name was originally spelled Kiesa and as a kid I really liked the s and the z. I liked that they look almost like a reflection. I just started spelling it that way and it stuck." As us Polish folks seem to have a problem with the s and z combination, not so with "Kiesza!"

You know him for rock'n songs such as "The Heart of Rock & Roll" and "The Power of Love," Hugh Anthony Cregg III, also known as Huey Lewis, singer, song writer, and leader of the rock group Huey Lewis and the News has, according to Ethnicelebs.com, a Polish mom. "He is the son of Maria Magdalena (Barcinski)... his mother was Polish, from Warsaw." The Polish rockers just keep popping up.

The February edition of the Polish American Journal referenced a Netflix multi-part documentary called "Medal of Honor" that began by highlighting the heroism of World War II Army Sergeant Sylvester Antolak. The series is excellent and the episode on Antolak shows incredible courage and a man with a strong Polish background.

As I listen to the news about President Trump's visit with North Korean leader Kim Jong Un there is also a lot of talk about the Korean War. That made me ponder on whether there were any Polish American Medal of Honor winners in that conflict. I found at least one with an obvious Polish name on the list. His name is Edward C. Krzyzowski, born in Chicago, Illinois in 1914, and he achieved the rank of captain. Captain Krzyzowski fought in World War II as well as Korea. Here is what he did to be awarded the United States "highest and most prestigious personal military decoration."

Capt. Krzyzowski, distinguished himself by conspicuous gallantry and indomitable courage above and beyond the call of duty in action against the enemy as commanding officer of Company B. Spearheading an assault against strongly defended Hill 700, his company came under vicious crossfire and grenade attack from enemy bunkers. Creeping up the fire-swept hill, he personally eliminated 1 bunker with his grenades and wiped out a second with carbine fire. Forced to retire to more tenable positions for the night, the company, led by Capt. Krzyzowski, resumed the attack the following day, gaining several hundred yards and inflicting numerous casualties. Overwhelmed by the numerically superior hostile force, he ordered his men to evacuate the wounded and move back. Providing protective fire for their safe withdrawal, he was wounded again by grenade fragments, but refused evacuation and continued to direct the defense. On September 3, he led his valiant unit in another assault which overran several hostile positions, but again the company was pinned down by murderous fire. Courageously advancing alone to an open knoll to plot mortar concentrations against the hill, he was killed instantly by an enemy sniper's fire.

We talk a lot about what it means to be Polish and the feeling of satisfaction, happiness, and responsibility that comes with it. When you read stories like this, you must feel the same and more for the Polish, but also the same and more as an American. We owe so much for those who fought on our behalf. I would like to confirm though, is Capt. Ed Krzyzowski, Polish or Not?

Wesolego Alleluja and wishing you a blessed and joy filled Easter! Our Polish babka plays a big part in the Swieconka dinner and if you are looking for some different looks and tastes at this year's gathering, check out the Zakopianski Rye and Poznanski Dark Rye loaves and others available at Future Bakery (https://www.futurebakery.com/polish-breads). Yum!

May 2019

Born in Poland

"Cop: Oh, yeah. Who the hell are you? Where you from?

Max: The Bronx

Cop: And you give away watches… and who gave it to you?

Max: My uncle Nathan…

Noodles: My little brother.

Cop: Tell your uncle to stop by the precinct.

Max: He's dead. Alcoholic. Ketrzyn, Poland.

Cop: Hm. Then he don't need it no more. It's been requisitioned."

— From the 1984 film, Once Upon a Time in America.

Noodles" is David Aaronson and "Max" is Maximilian Bercovicz and this scene is about a stolen watch which has been "requisitioned." You can decide what "requisitioned" means and it would not be surprising that a bunch of rascals of Jewish background roaming the streets in the lower East side of Manhattan at the turn of the 20th century in this country would reference Poland as their uncle's (real or not) place of birth. At the start of the Second World War about 3.5 million Jews were citizens of Poland and many others lived in Lithuania and Ukraine, two countries if not always controlled politically by Poland, were influenced by her socially and culturally for hundreds of years.

Considering how many Jews called Poland home at one time or another it probably would not be surprising at how many successful and important Americans of Jewish descent trace a generational home to Poland and some were even first generation immigrants from that nation. There are different list categories for Jewish Americans in Wikipedia and there is an exceptionally long one for "businesspeople." This list designates which individuals of Jewish descent and in business that were born in a country other than the United States. I did not add up how many have the "Born in Poland" tag but I am guessing it is at or near the highest number. Some of these folks you are most likely familiar with and others not so much. Here are a few of those "not so much" you might be interested in learning about.

Leo Gerstenzang – We start with Leo because he is the inventor of the Q-Tip! I write a lot about Poles who create or invent things because I am impressed with this ability and now we have another. Besides that, Q-Tips are something extremely useful to me because of my waxy ears.

"Gerstenzang was born in Warsaw… and he emigrated to Chicago, Illinois in 1912." In case you are wondering, the "Q" in Q-Tips stands for quality.

Maksymilian Faktorowicz – He is best known as Max Factor and along with Helena Rubinstein his name was another that I was most familiar with as a child for cosmetics advertisements on television. Faktorowicz was born September 15, 1877 in Zdunska Wola in pre-independence Congress Poland to Abraham Faktorowicz and Cecylia Wroclawska. He "popularized the term 'make-up' and was known for giving "signature looks" to actresses such as Jean Harlow, Clara Bow, Lucille Ball, and Joan Crawford.

Jack J. Grynberg – Jack Grynberg, born 1932, "is a Polish-born American businessman and developer in the oil and natural gas industry." He was "born to a Jewish family in Brest, Belarus, then part of Poland." Mr. Grynberg is a survivor of World War II, moved to American shortly after the war, earned his first million dollars at age 30, and continued to be "engaged in several successful domestic and international oil and gas exploration programs."

Leo Melamed – Mr. Melamed was born in Bialystok, Poland in 1932. When Poland was invaded his family fled to Lithuania and eventually across Siberia to Japan to avoid capture by the Germans. He immigrated to the United States in 1941 and settled in Chicago. Leo Melamed is "a pioneer of financial futures. He is the chairman emeritus of CME Group (formerly the Chicago Mercantile Exchange.)"

Paul Kalmanovitz – Kalmanovitz (originally Kalmanowicz) "a millionaire brewing and real estate magnate best known for owning all or part of several national breweries and products, including Falstaff Brewing Company and

Pabst Brewing Company. Most of the Kalmanovitz Estate was left to create a charitable foundation for hospitals and universities." He was born in Lodz, Poland in 1905 and although he moved to the United States before World War II, his brother Joseph died at Auschwitz.

Benjamin Winter – Ben Winter, also born in Lodz, Poland, February 5, 1881, gained success as a real estate developer and "served as president of the American Federation of Polish Jews." He is known for creating Fifth Avenue in New York City as the shopping mecca we know and owns properties such as Hotel Delmonico, the Stanhope Hotel, Bretton Hall, the Gunther Building, and the Hotel Claridge, among others.

Someone might ask, why is it important to note whether a Jew or anyone else except for a native Slavic Pole emigrated from Poland? I would say, even if a person (in this case) of Jewish ancestry lived in a totally contained ghetto somewhere in Poland, the fact that they lived and existed for a substantial period of time indicates that, at the least, they were able to assuage some benefit or good out of that experience.

That is a reflection, not on the person, but on the local community, the region, the state, or the nation in which they lived. People do not stay in places that are not safe or sustaining. So, when Gerstenzang, or Faktorowicz, or Winter says, "Where I come from… " you can say, "We come from the same place."

Polish or Not?

The first-ever champion of the Augusta National Women's Amateur golf tournament is Jennifer Kupcho, a student and member of the Wake Forest University golf team. "The event was established to inspire greater interest and participation in the women's game by creating a new, exciting and rewarding pathway for these players to fulfill their dreams." Jennifer also was the individual champion in the 2018 NCAA Division I Women's Golf championship. What a great match at Augusta National! Her name is like "Kupchak" (as in Polish American Sports Hall of Famer Mitch Kupchak) and that is why I ask, is Jennifer Kupcho, Polish or Not?

Broadcasting the inaugural Augusta National Women's Amateur was Steve Burkowski, "a reporter and producer for Golf Central, covering amateur events and the college golf ranks for the network." Whether Steve is Polish or not, I think it is neat to have a "Burkowski" in the broadcast booth. Perhaps one day he will move on and be doing PGA events. Move over Dan Hicks!

Also pertaining to the Division I NCAA Golf Championship, I noticed the individual champion winner in 2005 was Duke University's Anna Grzebien. This four-time All-American in golf won many other awards during her college career. After a five-year stint in the Ladies Professional Golf Association (LPGA), she hung it up on the tour for employment in the private sector. I remember seeing the name in some LPGA tourneys but did not realize her prowess during college. Is Anna, Polish or not and should Anna be included in the Polish American Sports Hall of Fame?

Since May is Polish Constitution month, I thought it would be appropriate to mention the Polish "Thermopylae," *The Battle of Hodow.* Thermopylae is where the Greek 300 Spartans defended a narrow passage against a huge invading Persian army. *The Battle of Hodow* was "between the Kingdom of Poland and Crimean Khanate forces, fought in June 1694." Polish strength was around 400 soldiers led by General Konstanty Zaborowski and the Khanate army had a troop strength estimated to be 40,000. Polish losses were 100 and the Crimean Khanate lost between 1000-2000 men. Check out Wikipedia for more information about this historical Polish military event and be sure to toast the Polish Sejm (parliament) of 1791 along with the Hodow 400!

June 2019

"Start with the Positive Things."

*T*hat quote and advice comes from Count Adam Zamoyski and to start with something positive I want to wish my mom, Audrey Lamczyk Poniewaz Mueller a heartfelt Sto Lat!! as she is now 89 years young. What a life and what a great woman. I love you mother dear and thank you for everything you have done for me and our family. God bless you.

The name Adam Zamoyski is familiar to many if not most of us. There are famous doers and then there are chroniclers and he fits very nicely into the latter category. Adam has written fifteen books and has been a contributor or author on other publications mostly on the subject of Poland. He is a passionate man of incredible intellect and insight and is one of a small number of writers or researchers that have made a specific and major impact by documenting our history and culture. His latest book is *Napoleon: The Man Behind the Myth* (2018, London, William Collins).

We read the books but what about the person writing them? I was struck watching a YouTube interview with him in a segment called "Heart of Poland," sponsored by Project Kazimierz (https://projectkazimierz.com) and produced and moderated by Patrick Ney. More on Mr. Ney later but please see this program as Zamoyski addresses a number of questions about his family, his personal background and development, how his interest in Poland began, his understanding of the Polish character, Polish-Jewish relations, and "the ways Poles talk and reflect on their difficult past."

One of the highlights of the talk should register for those of us of Polish ancestry that grew up in another culture as did Zamoyski, a British citizen since the 1940s. What he says nicely encapsulates the approach to national identity for an immigrant family, by his immigrant family, and how that shaped his perspective as a historian.

Our Polishness was not something special and hidden, a kind of faith that one has to worship, it was the natural part of the European heritage and as a result I think it has helped me enormously when I write about Polish subjects and Polish history, because so many people who write about Polish history, whether they are Poles or whether they are foreigners, I mean look at Norman Davies, they get tremendously sentimental, emotional about the whole thing and they are either fighting in the Polish corner or they are saying the Poles are frightful.

This feeling is from someone who obviously loves being Polish and has great admiration for the people and country of Poland but as a historian is neutral on the final determination. Too, immigrants or refugees living in a foreign land often dismiss or hide their "difference" rather than, as Zamoyski explains, treat it as a natural part of a regional or world experience.

I wish I had his words instilled in me as a young boy. I think I would have had a better understanding of my worth and a more comfortable relationship to the community around me. America it seems has had such a pecking order when it comes to identity and we still are grappling with it today. Maybe this video will help you grapple with it as well. You can see it by searching "Adam Zamoyski Heart of Poland YouTube."

Now about Patrick Ney. Incredible!! You will find a bio on him on the Project Kazimierz website. Like Adam Zamoyski, Patrick is a British citizen in a love affair with the country of Poland, yet he had no Polish connection until a decade ago. Since 2010 he has been living in Poland and is a filmmaker and writer and "his films focus on Polish society and history. They have had more than 23 million views in the last 12 months."

There's so much going on in Poland,' he says, 'it's this cauldron of dynamism, hard work and opportunity. Living here has changed me…

Imagine that. Two men of English nationality were impressed and hooked by this mysterious place set in the middle of the European continent. Those of us that also got the bug for things Polish understand this as well. Check out Project Kazimierz for an exciting look into the new Poland.

Polish or Not?

There is an article entitled "The 50 Sexiest Women You've Probably Never Heard Of" (http://whatculture.com/tv/50-sexiest-women-youve-probably-never-heard-of) and of course I had to check to see how many of the "never heard of" are Polish. The one that is specifically identified as Polish is the lead singer for the American rock band *Yeah Yeah Yeahs,* Karen O. Her real name is Karen Lee Orzolek and she was born in South Korea to a Polish father and a Korean mother. Besides being a singer and performer, Karen is known for her fashion statements, her theatrics on stage, soundtrack work, and collaboration with filmmaker Spike Jonze. Beautiful and talented, half-Polish Karen "O" Orzolek. Now you've heard of her.

Bob Huggins is the coach of the West Virginia University men's basketball team. He previously coached for the University of Cincinnati and his combined success at both colleges is quite impressive as he has racked up 859 wins in his career. He has a very Slavic looking face and was born in West Virginia, a state with a substantial Eastern European population. Does Bob "Huggy Bear" Huggins have a Polish connection, or not?

We have a lot of "movements" currently: Antifa, Me Too, Descendants of Slavery Reparations, and WalkAway. The WalkAway Campaign encourages members of the Democrat party to "walk away" if they feel that the policies, positions, and mission of the party do not adequately represent them. The leader of this movement is Brandon Straka who grew up in Nebraska, bears a striking resemblance to Richie Sambora (the former lead guitarist of the rock band Bon Jovi), and has a Slavic-looking name. Is Brandon Polish or Not?

Just in, Miss USA 2019 is Chelsie Kryst whose dad is white and mother is African American. When the ethnicity of the "white" parent is not specified, often that is a good indication that the parent might be Polish. Add to that, is "Kryst" a shortened version of say, "Krystkowiak" as in Larry Krystkowiak, coach of the NCAA University of Utah men's basketball team? Could Miss USA 2019, Chelsie Kryst, be Polish, or not?

Solareye (www.sOlareye.biz) is a communications company based in Irvine, California run by Leonard and Basia Myszynski. These "Image Makers and Story Tellers" are Polish born emigres that have produced several films and their latest is the documentary *Bridging Urban America: The Story of Ralph Modjeski* (http://bridginguamericafilm.com). I saw this film and met Basia and Leonard. Modjeski, along with the Myszynskis are very impressive and I recommend you check out Solareye and watch this documentary.

July 2019

The Study of "Us."

A young man in our circle of family and friends told me that his major is anthropology and that is a field of study that hasn't been heard of in a long time. With all the talk about the low pay and unemployability of the arts versus the sciences especially when adjusted for the cost (debt) of the degree, I was surprised to hear it.

It did remind me though of my time as an undergrad and the classes needed to fulfill "electives" along with the required courses in Business Administration. My brilliant advisor picked good professors especially over the subjects and I was thankful for the one he recommended that taught Cultural Anthropology. I told the young man with the major how much I enjoyed my anthropology course 45 years ago and how it aligned with my journey in discovering my ancestry.

"Cultural anthropology is a branch of anthropology focused on the study of cultural variation among humans" and three of the big names tossed around in my class were Franz Boaz, Margaret Mead, and Polish born Bronislaw Malinowski. Boaz established an empirical approach to anthropology, Mead explained how individual personalities were influenced by the larger culture and society, and Malinowski was famous for introducing the documentation of cultural details through participant observation and fieldwork.

One of the assignments I had in this class was to create a family tree by interviewing key members of my family. That exercise helped give me a glimpse into our family's immigrant experience and that lead to doing oral histories of other Poles and their experiences. It was fascinating stuff and please, please document the lives of the older members of your family. Even the smallest and innocuous details are important.

Malinowski is an important figure in the field of anthropology and there are a number of his countrymen and women that have excelled in this academic discipline as well. Their personal lives are quite intriguing, and it seems as

if they were drawn into their vocations and pursuits based on those experiences. A web site you can consult to find out more about some of these
"other" Polish anthropologists is Culture.Pl (https://culture.pl/en/article/
more-than-malinowski-polish-cultural-anthropologists).

For instance, Maria Czaplicka (1884-1921) was a contemporary of Malinowski and she gained attention for her anthropological research of the subject
matter from existing published sources. Her most famous project though was
leading an expedition to Siberia (named Yenisei) to study and document the
Tungusic people. She was the first woman to lecture at Oxford University
and became "politically involved in the suffrage movement, as well as in
matters concerning the fight for Poland's independence."

In a similar way, the seed of resistance in Czaplicka was also found in the
heart of Bronislaw Pilsudski (1866-1918 and the brother of Marshall Jozef
Pilsudski) as he leapfrogged from insurrectionist to anthropologist. His story
starts as a prisoner of the Russian Czar Alexander II on Sakhalin Island in
the Pacific. By chance it was suggested by another ethnographer imprisoned
with him "to study the culture of the Ainu people, who inhabited Sakhalin
and the islands of Northern Japan." Pilsudski is acknowledged for his use
of photographs and sound recordings in his research. In modern times the
Ainus have been assimilated into the general Japanese population and they
have relied on Pilsudski's research photos and recordings to recapture their
ancestral uniqueness.

Like Czaplicka and Pilsudski, Jan Kubary began his adult life in the cause
of independence for his country and gravitated to the study of cultures and
anthropology. After the Polish rebellion of 1863, the "January Uprising," he
left for Germany where he worked in a natural history museum. It was this
job that gave him the incentive and opportunity to travel to Oceania and this
became his new home. While Kubary did not have the academic background
to support his writings and research, what he did have was the devotion to
and compassion for the people he lived with. His body of work is important
and a testament to this approach as stated in *Culture:*

*His research in Oceania was unprecedented, although he was self-
taught, having left Europe equipped with no background in ethnography whatsoever. In his 28 years among the Papuan people, he
integrated with local communities and gained competence in their
languages. Apart from ethnographic works, Kubary left behind many*

geographical and natural reports, as well as an impressive collection of items, which are now housed in European museums.

Modern ethnography, anthropology, and cultural anthropology as academic pursuits largely took off during the 19th century and perhaps so many of the well-known Polish anthropologists started their careers during this period because their own culture was being appropriated by invaders and partitioning nations. Freedom allows us time for introspection and enjoyment of who we are. Slavery and oppression, whether of the mind, spirit, or body, takes that sense away from us. Perhaps that is the best reason we have for at least one young person in the world pursue this course of study.

Polish or Not?

Do you remember the bubblegum sounds of the 60's and in particular the 1910 Fruitgum Company? I do and had a lot of fun bopping to their tunes because it was the kind of rock that appealed to teenagers of that era. Fruitgum had hits like "Simon Says," "1, 2, 3, Red Light," "Goody, Goody, Gumdrops," and "Indian Giver."

The original band members were from Linden, New Jersey and the voice you heard on all of the hits was Mark Gutkowski, who as well as being the lead singer played the Hammond B3 organ and, if I am not mistaken, in some of the early videos of the band, he is seen playing the guitar as well. He, his brother Ted, and band member Frank Jeckell wrote all the songs for the "Indian Giver" album.

I am putting Mark and Ted down for Polish but if a reader knows otherwise, what happened to them, or if there are other Polish connections among the original members, please share. Polish or not for Gutkowski and what happened to him after 1910 Fruitgum?

On a recent episode of *Fox News Sunday* with Chris Wallace the "Power Player of the Week" was the award-winning history writer Robert Caro. He is perhaps the best or among the best authorities on the life of former president Lyndon Johnson. According to Wikipedia, Caro's father, Benjamin Caro, was born in Warsaw, Poland.

Penske or Penski? If you watched one of the most exciting Indy 500 races in recent years you could not help hearing the name Penske mentioned numerous times. Roger Penske is head of one if not the winningest NASCAR and IndyCar Series teams in history. He "is the most successful owner in the Indianapolis 500 with 18 victories." Some of you might get this: If George Costanza is not "Penske" material, Roger Penske certainly is. I could not resist.

Born February 20, 1937 in Shaker Heights, Ohio, Penske grew up in Cleveland and began fixing up older cars as a teenager and at age 82 is now a billionaire. So, is Roger Penske (Penski), Polish or Not?

Of "all time" is the kind of adjective we look for and like to advertise in The Pondering Pole and in this case, it is assigned to John Brzenk, professional arm-wrestler. He was born July 15, 1964 in McHenry, Illinois, is retired now due to injuries, and according to Arm-wrestling.com (https://arm-wrestling.fandom.com/wiki/John_Brzenk) "it is estimated that John has won over 500 titles in his career" and he is "widely recognized as the greatest arm-wrestler of all time." Is John "Giant Crusher" Brzenk, Polish or Not?

August 2019

Reparations or Restorations?

*I*n the June 2019 issue of *Catalyst,* the journal for the Catholic League for Religious and Civil Rights, President William Donohue asks in his regular "From the President's Desk" editorial, "How much do I owe Oprah?" The editorial is about the current discussion (and some would say politics) of "reparations to African Americans because their ancestors were enslaved." You can read the piece yourself on the position he presents, but in it was the mention of the discrimination of Southern and Eastern Europeans, "particularly those of Polish extraction… in the Immigration Acts of 1921 and 1924."

I was not aware of the 1921 and 1924 Immigration Acts and Dr. Donohue went through a litany of other groups that have in one time or another encountered discrimination and bigotry. My father used to tell the story about a company in Saint Louis that would not hire Catholics. In at least two or three company sponsored "how not to discriminate" programs and workshops I attended in my career, "Polish employees" was an example specifically mentioned because businesses were afraid of being sued for derogatory bias. Based on all the social unkindness we have endured for so many years I always felt good about this. I really do believe our people have been held back by ignorant or mean-spirited persons or philosophies but does anyone or anything owe us?

As this is written around the July 4th celebrations there is a lot of talk about the American Dream. At least one definition says this is "the set of ideals (democracy, rights, liberty, opportunity and equality) in which freedom includes the opportunity for prosperity and success, as well as an upward social mobility for the family and children, achieved through hard work in a society with few barriers." That is lofty and powerful stuff. Legal protections are of course important and needed but in the "who owes" category, at least for Poles as Americans, the "Dream" should be balanced against the injuries, and the "Dream" wins out. Nobody owes you anything; shake it off, don't look back, and excel.

One great way to excel is to show 'em what you've got, or in the case of Swiatek Studios Inc., repair and restore what you have created in the past, and this applies in many cases to you 1921 and 1924 immigrants. Swiatek has been around since 1967, started by Henry Swiatek Sr., and is now being continued with his son Henry Jr., his grandson Brett, and his daughter Stacey Swiatek by restoring historic buildings, churches, and homes. They also do faux painting services and their territory is primarily in the Northeast part of the United States.

From the website:

The Studio is well known for our specialization in high-level architectural restoration projects, craftsmanship, historic conservation, decorative painting, statue restoration, plastering, and stained-glass repair and restoration. We passionately apply our collective knowledge to each and every project and focus on the design and production of quality artwork. You can see the results of this dedication in our work.

Henry Swiatek told me in a phone conversation that so many of our Polish churches in the United States are "cathedral like." He is right. What greater expression of the American Dream is the beautiful and significant work by Swiatek Studios. Check them out online (http://www.swiatekstudios.com) and be amazed at what they do!

Polish or Not?

Another Polish model and this one is for the ladies. Francisco Lachowski was born in Brazil to a Polish father and a German and Portuguese mom (https://ethnicelebs.com/francisco-lachowski). Like a lot of the most famous runway walkers, Lachowski began his career by competing and winning "Ford Models Supermodel of the World" contest. Some of the designer labels he has worked for include Gucci, Dior, Versace, Armani, and has made the cover for some of the top fashion magazines. "In 2015, models.com included Lachowski on their 'Industry Icons' and 'Sexiest Men' lists."

"Clematis" is from the Greek word meaning "a climbing plant" and the different kinds are "often named for their originators or particular characteristics." One kind of Clematis is called "The Polish Spirit" and it is called that because it was "bred by Brother Stefan Franczak, a monk who for more than 50 years has been gardener at the Jesuit Theological College in Warsaw."

Here is a brief description of the vine from the Gardeners World website (https://www.gardenersworld.com/plants/clematis-polish-spirit):

Clematis 'Polish Spirit' bears rich purple-blue flowers from mid-summer to early autumn. Growth is very vigorous and the plant retains its foliage well throughout the season. It is perfect for growing up a trellis or fence and may also be trained to scramble through trees and shrubs. A viticella clematis, it shows good resistance to clematis wilt.

"Polish Spirit" is one of 70 species of Clematis that has won the Royal Horticultural Society's Award of Garden Merit for "this plant's continued popularity in gardens in the United Kingdom." Check it out and more important, grow one.

A new Polish vodka discovery! On *The First News* website (https://www. thefirstnews.com) is a story about innovators in something the Poles excel at and that is the making of vodka. The name of the company is Frant (https:// frantvodka.com), which produces "a collection of niche, high-end vodkas and spirits from Poland." The brains behind Frant are Dorota Zylewicz-Nosowska and Filip Pagowski.

Dorota is described as "a long-time industry professional and all-around spirits nerd." Reading her impressive business bio, it is apparent she is the kind of person that throws herself completely into the project, doing the research with an eye for detail, and going for the exceptional product. She manages the operation, product development, export, and sales for Frant.

Filip is "a renowned graphic artist working between Warsaw and New York who co-designed Frant's brand identity." According to his bio on the Frant website, Filip created the "PLAY" icon (that little triangle pointing to the right) that tells us to play the video, movie, or song on our phone, television, or other device. You have seen many variations on this click in your life. His father is the "legendary poster artist Henryk Tomaszewski."

One product that Frant has developed is Wildflower, "a dry spirit distilled entirely from wildflower honey collected from the pristine Warmia-Mazurian fields." Sounds like a lighter version of Krupnik with a vodka taste and twist. Unfortunately, Frant vodka is not yet available in the United States but per Dorota, "I am working on it." Hurry up Dorota!!

September 2019

In Heaven, There Must Be Chupaj Siupaj

"The company pairs off quickly, and the whole room is soon in motion… there is music, and they dance, each as he pleases, just as before they sang. Most of them prefer the "two-step," especially the young, with whom it is the fashion. The older people have dances from home, strange and complicated steps which they execute with grave solemnity."

— Upton Sinclair, The Jungle

Okay, another bucket-list experience. I have never been to a polka "fest", but I did sign on to attend the Pulaski Polka Days in Pulaski, Wisconsin July 18-21 (as advertised in the Polish American Journal). My wife Sue and I were there with our friends from California, Andy and Liz Kozlowski, and if you enjoy polka music and dance and you can make it next year, go.

I will never be an oom pah pah-er; I will never be a Slovenian slider; in my heart I am a hopper true and true and this festival is filled with Polish-style bangers and blasters. The dancers on display were amazing. Their ages ranged from eight to eighty. The sights, smells, and sounds were wonderful and as Andy said, "I just feel so at home here." It was about a hundred degrees on Friday and everyone was soaked with sweat and then a storm came through and blew out the lights. But only for time and everything was back up and cranking on Saturday. The good times rolled on.

There were highlights. The Polka Country Musicians (https://www.polkacountry.com) do the standard brass and accordion motif but they also switch to fiddles to power the rhythm and I gotta tell you, it has a super old-time and folksy kind of sound that works perfectly in the Polish dance style. If you are Irish or want to be Irish, you might hear familiar melodies from the Country Musicians that fit for you as well. It was wonderful music and presence by these guys.

Box On (http://boxonband.com) is a family-membered group out of Michigan that, as their website states, presents "a new generation of music." That is true and the star of the show is the lead singer Alex Vinecki who is a consummate showman and watching him on stage reminds me of another passage about the leader of the band from *The Jungle:*

For he is an inspired man. Every inch of him is inspired – you might almost say inspired separately. He stamps with his feet, he tosses his head, he sways and swings to and fro… when he executes a turn or a flourish, his brows knit and his lips work and his eyelids wink… and every now and then he turns upon his companions, nodding, signaling, beckoning frantically – with every inch of him appealing, imploring, in behalf of the muses and their call.

That is Alex and although he does seem possessed by an inner calling he plays, dances, and sings passionately for his audience. (You can watch him on YouTube at https://www.youtube.com/watch?v=1XNlaEUilQs).

So, there are the Osmonds, the Jacksons, and now the Vineckis, a family that plays together, stays together, and is on a mission to expand, create, and excite. From what I could see, their fans believe it and they know how to get them hopping.

While in Pulaski, be sure you stop in to see the Assumption of the Blessed Virgin Mary Catholic Church. Pulaski has a population of 3500 residents. I do not know if there are any other churches in the town but for the Catholics, they built, as Henry Swiatek would say (Pondering Pole August 2019), something "cathedral like." If you like old Polish churches, it is big and beautiful.

Polish or Not?

There is a show on Netflix called *Blown Away* about a competition for glass blowing and Janusz Pozniak was one of the artists in the field. His reputation precedes him based on the comments by the other contestants and if you check out his website you will see why (https://www.januszpozniak.com).

The 53-year-old Pozniak, born in the United Kingdom, is Polish on his dad's side and he began "working with glass when he was 19." He has won numerous awards and has worked with several well-known glass artists including the great Dale Chihuly. Pozniak's method and pieces have been explained as "pushing the boundaries beyond form and function to abstractly reflect his own personal experiences and distill human emotion." Watch *Blown Away* and see him in action pushing boundaries.

From the website www.zloz.com, Neil Zlozower is "Widely considered one of the greatest music photographers of all time… "

He has shot "iconic" photos of Van Halen, Led Zeppelin, Guns N' Roses, and many other rock stars and bands. His work has appeared on hundreds of magazine and album covers. You can find some of his pictures on www. atlasicons.com. Cannot find much in the way of a bio on him, so is Neil "Zlozowski" Zlozower, Polish, or not?

October 2019

Bitter or Better?

*T*his alliteration (there was another "B," for butter, "everything's better with Blue Bonnet on it!") came from the sermon at Mass, Labor Day weekend, and the priest was talking about whether our work and life consists mainly of bitterness and disappointment or are we always thinking that what we do makes life better for ourselves and for others. He tied it to the Gospel message in this way: if you love God, love your neighbor, and especially important, if you love yourself, then your life cannot be filled with bitterness. Those rules can only point us in the direction of making life better for ourselves and others.

If you are Polish, sometimes it is hard not to fall into frustration, disappointment, and, unfortunately, bitterness. We hear and read the criticism leveled at Poles over and over again for their role in World War II, the political and social tumult going on in that country (some of it true but mostly fake news), and of the diminishing participation, presence, and awareness of Polonia in this country. You can probably add your own disappointments to these.

For any of the bitterness we encounter remember there is usually the flip side. The Poles performance in World War II was heroic, the modern Poland on balance is a stable, productive, and energized country, and while the excitement and newness of immigration has worn off for most Polish-Americans, those still living and enjoying adherence to or promotion of Polish culture are probably more dedicated and mature in their approach, consciousness, and willingness to contribute or participate.

For the most part, Poles in the U.S. or at home in Poland are more educated, secure, freer, and richer probably than they have ever been. The Wikipedia listing of ethnic groups by household income (2016 data) shows Polish Americans with a median income of $71,172 or 29th place out of 97 groups that were reported (https://en.wikipedia.org/wiki/List_of_ethnic_groups_in_the_United_States_by_household_income). Average wages (2017 data) in Poland are among the highest in Eastern Europe (https://en.wikipedia.org/

wiki/List_of_countries_by_average_wage). If there is nothing else to cheer about, at least the one thing we can hold dear is that if we were dreaming of a better life then we have achieved it. Because we've achieved it, the overall society is the better for it as well.

In another Wiki post and an example of the stats just stated, there is billionaire Edward P. Roski Jr. who is the son of Ed Roski Sr. who "was the son of a poor immigrant family from Poland who did not finish high school. Roski Sr. served in the United States Navy during World War II, and then moved the family to Southern California, where he founded Majestic Realty in 1948." Sr. did not finish high school but started what eventually became a giant real-estate company.

Ed Jr. picked up where dad left off and took over the reins of Majestic and he now owns "more than 83 million square feet of real estate across the United States." He is the owner of multiple pro sports teams and perhaps his greatest claim to fame is his role as co-developer of the Staples Center in downtown Los Angeles. You can explore more to this man's fabulous life and I'm guessing you will find the thread that ran through it was not bitterness but optimism and a desire to make things better for himself and those around him. Isn't that the better choice?

Polish or Not?

Did'ja ever wonder what is the difference between a kosher pickle and a Polish pickle? I'm neither a big sweet pickle fan nor do I like the Bread N' Butter pickles but give me the Kosher-Polish "type" in all the varieties they come in. The roots of both come from the same place and there are various explanations for why they are different on the web. Here is a summary from the *Our Everyday Life* site about these pickles (https://oureverydaylife.com/kosher-pickle-vs-polish-pickle-40645.html).

Kosher is more about the flavor than anything to do with Jewish religious laws. Generally, they have more garlic added to the traditional dill flavors. Polish "dills contain more spices and garlic than either traditional dill pickles or kosher dill pickles." Some of the spices added are a combination of peppers and mustard seed.

For me, Polish pickles from the regular grocery stores do have more of a kick and are crunchier than the Kosher. Those purchased from ethnic or specialty outlets are dillier, less peppery, and softer. My Grandma's from the farm had a strong vinegar and salt taste and were delicious. Try a taste test of your own or if you have a brand of Polish pickles that are your favorite let me know what you think.

For the record, the Nathan of Nathan's Famous brand and the Coney Island hotdog eating contest was started in 1916 by Polish immigrant Nathan Handwerker. Besides hotdogs, Nathan's makes a pretty fine pickle.

A person you most probably know but has been popping up on the ticker quite a bit lately is the exceeding beautiful actress Yvonne Strahovski. Born July 30, 1982, her real name is Yvonne Jacqueline Strzechowski. You probably were introduced to her as the character Sarah Walker in the series *Chuck*. Yvonne has gotten a lot of work in film and television since *Chuck* and her most recent television series is *The Handmaid's Tale* "for which she has received a Primetime Emmy Award nomination." It seems Yvonne is getting better and better in her career and we are happy for her.

November 2019

Definitely Not Commando

*T*his will be forever known as the Pondering Pole underwear edition.

Beginning it seems in the 70s and 80s there has been a lot of underwear and lingerie advertising with Hanes, Fruit of the Loom, Fredericks of Hollywood, and Victoria's Secret as the old standbys and now brands like Duluth Trading, Tommy John, and a myriad of other innovative and startup undergarment and lingerie businesses are doing great work in this industry. Yes, there is an "undies" industry.

So, is there a Polish connection? There is at least one. Olga is the brand name of intimate women's wear founded in America by Polish-born Olga Erteszek. She was born in Krakow, Poland in 1916, and grew up working for her mother who was a corsetiere, someone "who specializes in making, fitting, or selling corsets, brassieres, or other foundation garments." Olga, along with her husband Jan, fled Poland after the German invasion in World War II and eventually made their way to the United States and settled in California with Olga finding work as a seamstress making girdles and bras.

While at the garment factory and according to Wikipedia, "One day she spotted a woman on a trolley with hosiery rolled to her knees. She said to Jan that it was a shame that women didn't have at least some bit of finery to hold up their stockings… " The garter she created to solve the problem allowed her and Jan to go into business making them. Demand grew and the company, named for her, blossomed.

Olga Erteszek was an innovator, designer, and a businesswoman. "Holding the woman's record for patents at 28, Olga brought woman many pleasing, comfortable, and fashionable undergarments." Her signature piece is the nightgown with a "full flowing shirt width and generous sweep."

Olga was one of the first companies to begin profit sharing for their employees and Erteszek and Jan won several awards for their humanitarian endeavors. "In 1984, Olga was ranked as a Fortune 500 company and one of the best companies to work for in America." She died September 15, 1989 but the business lives on as a product line of the Warnaco Company. Quite a woman and guys, get your wife or girlfriend an Olga gift card for that special occasion!

Although this next story is about "outer" wear, it is a related one worth telling. Biba is the name of a women's fashion store in London, England, no longer in business but popular during the 1960s and 70s. Biba was the brainchild of Polish-born Barbara Hulanicki. "Biba" is a nickname for Barbara Hulanicki's younger sister Biruta. She chose it (and I love the choice) as the name of her clothing store in 1960s London which "she started and primarily ran… with the help of her husband Stephen Fitz-Simon."

Barbara's background was in fashion illustration. After she married Stephen Fitz-Simon, they "opened a mail order clothing company that she named Biba's Postal Boutique." The mail order company became a brick and mortar shop in Kensington in London's West End in 1964. The big break came when the store offered a super stylish dress.

Biba's postal boutique had its first significant success in May 1964 when it offered a pink gingham dress with a hole cut out of the back of the neck with a matching triangular kerchief to readers of the **Daily Mirror**. *The dress had celebrity appeal, as a similar dress had been worn by Brigitte Bardot. By the morning after the dress was advertised in the* **Daily Mirror**, *over 4,000 orders had been received. Ultimately, some 17,000 outfits were sold.*

Barbara Hulanicki's story, like Olga Erteszek, like most every other entrepreneur that ever lived is similar: they had a talent or passion and an idea, made the idea into reality, tested it, and then promoted and sold it in a market economy. These Polish ladies became successes in the market and their legacy lives on. In fact, some of us are wearing their legacy now.

Polish or Not?

Don Grolnick, born September 23, 1947 in Brooklyn, New York, was "an American jazz pianist, composer, and record producer." He was well-known as a session musician for famous music stars such as Roberta Flack, Harry Chapin, Carly Simon, and Steely Dan. According to Wikipedia, "he began his musical life on accordion but later switched to piano." Accordion huh? That caught my attention and is an interesting clue to whether Grolnick is Polish, or not?

Cleveland, Polish or Not? Of course, Polish! But you knew that. In the September 2019 edition of Southwest Airlines, *The Magazine* (found in the seat pocket with the card showing exits under your drop-down tray table), the city of Cleveland was featured, and two Polish connections were mentioned. First was a plug for Sokolowski's restaurant featuring their famous pierogi. "Sokolowski's claims to be the city's oldest family-owned restaurant… " It is on my bucket list to dine there some day.

The second was Brandon Chrostowski, the founder of Edwin's Leadership Institute & Restaurant, "a nonprofit education program for formerly incarcerated adults who want to build careers in the culinary and hospitality industries." Impressive guy doing God's work.

VI

Dziekuje Bardzo!

Dziekuje Bardzo

Dziekuje bardzo (pronunciation: jane-koo'-yeah bard'-zoe) in Polish means "thank you very much" and at the end of some Pondering Pole columns I acknowledge and thank people that provided leads or information that was useful and worth noting in the writing of the column.

I am listing those from 2016-2019 for the most part in their original form below and if I missed you forgive me for the oversight, but I am grateful you participated.

Besides those contributing with the articles, I also thank my family and the Saint Louis Polish community for their support and feedback. A big thank you to my son-in-law, Alex, for helping me put the book together. I want to especially thank my wife Sue. She often prodded and kept me on track: "Are finished with your article yet?" She also gave me great encouragement by honestly assessing and (almost always) liking what I wrote. That meant a lot.

Two people need special recognition. The first is the editor of the Polish American Journal Mark Kohan for giving me the opportunity to fulfill my quest to reveal Polish exceptionalism and excite the folks with thought-provoking ideas. The other is Jack Jackowski, a Polish American Journal reader from Michigan and my number one researcher supplying me with leads of important and successful Polish people, places, and events. At this point I consider him an associate, collaborator, and a good friend.

Here is the list of dziekuje bardzos from 2016 through 2019.

A big dziekuje bardzo to Frank J. Nice for sharing all the great work he is doing and to Sue Czerwinski for sharing Marek with us! Thanks to Jacek Jackowski for the lead on Conrad Prebys. Happy Valentine's Day and like little Marek, happiness and peace and love to all of you Pondering Poles out there. Say a prayer of thanks for having a home in this great country and for God to have mercy on the people in loveless and violent situations. We are blessed.

A big dziekuje bardzo to Mark, Tom, and Jack for the information on Frank "Popeye" Fiegel. Popeye is a Pole who said "I ams what I ams and that's all that I ams" and if you don't like it… Eat your spinach Polonians and put up your intellectual dukes.

Dziekuje bardzo to Rich Widerynski, Polish National Alliance member who gave me valuable information on Pola Negri and her involvement with Our Lady of the Bright Mount. Finally, I didn't catch her name but our waitress at the Polka restaurant in Los Angeles was exceedingly patient with us as we mixed and matched and ordered too much food. Dziekuje to her as well.

The start of summer!! Grill up a bunch of pork steaks and then wash 'em down at your favorite "meeting place." Dziekuje bardzo to Johnny Baras of the PNA, Nini Harris for information on The Stone Bar, Joe and Henry Mulnik for the history of Polish Hall, and Sto Lat! to Polish Halla and all of the many folks that have kept it open all of these years and those who were touched in one way or another by it.

A big dziekuje bardzo to Jack Jackowski for the great information on Conrad Prebys! Hope you are having a wonderful summer and enjoy the last two months. I say two months because with global warming September is now an extension of the summer season rather than the beginning of Fall. Around here anyway that is true. Just an FYI, the best golf in the Midwest is in September and October.

A lot of dziekujes are due. Thank you Mary Ann Roberts for the letter of kind words and the enclosed article about Eddie Basinski, the classically trained violin playing and scrappy second baseman of the Portland Beavers. What an interesting and talented guy. There probably will be more to come about Eddie for Pondering Pole readers in the future. Thank you, Brigette Poniewaz Schubert for the leads and links on *Marysia and Tula* and the Kielbasa Hash. Thank you, Katie at Lemon Poppy Kitchen for the background story and recipe for the Kielbasa Hash and creating a new Polish dish. I love hearing about new Polish culinary creations and it does sound delicious!

Dziekuje bardzo to Robert Ogrodnik, former Honorary Consul for the Republic of Poland, for arranging the visits to the locations and booking the accommodations for the Chicago tour and to Wojciech Golik for being our stellar tour leader. What a great trip!! Part the reason the Highlander children did such a great job is due to their instructor Marek Ogorek. Dziekuje bardzo and please keep up the good work Marek!!

Dziekuje Bardzo

Dziekuje Bardzo to Doctor Susan Gromacki Lathrop for the kind words and the lead on Alexander Lubomirski. Thanks also to Professor Ronald Rychlak for the perspective on the "Blue Police" and information on his family.

Big, big dziekuje bardzos to Norb Dzienciol, Margaret Zotkiewicz-Dramczyk, and John Ziobrowski for the excellent feedback and participation, and to Tony and Alice Kaminski for the Noah story. Maybe an extra special thanks to Tony and Alice for being such great grandparents to a wonderful boy like Noah!

I enjoyed receiving eMails from Dr. Frank Nice and Dr. Susan J. Gromacki. Thank you for the information about Neal Diamond and Britt Slabinski. Thanks to Greg and Janie for their impressions of Poland and their visit to the city of Krakow and for the great gifts. Finally, my personal dziekuje bardzo to Grzegorz Koltuniak and his wife Grazyna for their courage and sacrifice in the cause of freedom and for the betterment of their country. They are two of many heroes living among us.

Dziekuje bardzo to Dr. Susan Gromacki for the information on reps Kulik and Scibak.

Dziekuje bardzo to Mark Kohan for passing on a couple great Pondering Pole topics the past two months. Thank you, Henry Swiatek for the wonderful talk about our mutual love for old buildings. Nice to hear from Dorota Zylewicz-Nosowska and we are all praying you start shipping Frant vodka to the U.S. soon.

Thank you to Andy and Liz for a wonderful trip and experience. Let's do it again!!

Thank you Debbie Majka of the American Council for Polish Culture (ACPC) for the information regarding Yvonne Strahovski. Thank you as well for your leadership in the important work you have done with ACPC.

After reading The Pondering Pole, if you have a thought about any topic presented, have a question, or have interesting facts to share, eMail me alinabrig@yahoo.com.

N.B. If you send eMail, reference the Polish American Journal or the Pondering Pole in the subject line. I will not open an eMail if I do not recognize the subject or the sender.